## Acknowledgements

The extensive renovations to Somerset Park proved to be the catalyst for this book and I am grateful to Ayr United owner David Smith for being most co-operative in granting permission for the reproduction of plans that he had commissioned. Even the most descriptive narrative can require visual enhancement to truly bring it to life. More pertinent though is the fact that the changing face of the ground owes itself to his foresight. Without that foresight, and the practical application of it, the thought would never have occurred to write this book at all. I thank him too for taking time out of a busy schedule to check the last two chapters for accuracy.

Former Ayr United player David Kennedy is a grandson of John Muir who was conferred with an honorary life membership of the club for helping to drive substantial improvements to Somerset Park in the 1950s. David kindly supplied some very nostalgic photographs from that era. These show volunteers having a break from building the boundary wall in 1950, the opening of the gymnasium in 1952 and John Muir being presented with his honour in 1954. I thank David for this most valuable contribution from his family history files.

Without fear of contradiction it can be stated that no one possesses greater knowledge of the town of Ayr than Tom Barclay. In 2022 Tom retired from Carnegie Library after forty-seven years of service. With his breadth of knowledge it was no surprise to me when he answered my queries about historic locations of Ayr Cattle Market. Ayr Cattle Market? You may wonder at the relevance. Rather than wonder just read on. Agricultural matters actually did have a large bearing on the evolution of football in the town.

With digital now being the way of the world I have been happy to acquire a vast number of hard copies of photographs from the *Ayrshire Post* and the *Ayr Advertiser*. Some of those appear between these pages therefore they are deserving of acknowledgement here. I will forego my customary thanks to these newspapers for their unashamed Ayr United bias. To their credit that bias still exists but the subject matter here relates to the ground rather than the team.

Even when improvements continue apace, the Ayr United board tend to remain aware of the club's heritage therefore a key aspect of obtaining planning consents is a desire to be mindful of that heritage. Somerset Park will never be accused of lacking soul for as long as the current directors are custodians of the club. These directors are worthy of acknowledgement here. In addition to David Smith they are Fraser McIntyre, Graeme Mathie, Alan Murray and William Houston.

*Duncan Carmichael*
*Monkton*
*July 2023*

Old Lady Somerset

*Destruction was a necessary prelude to construction. The vast undertaking on the north terrace got underway in June 2023*

# Old Lady Somerset

*Ayr United
at Home*

Duncan Carmichael

Kennedy & Boyd,
an imprint of
Zeticula Ltd,
Unit 13,
196 Rose Street,
Edinburgh,
EH2 4AT,
Scotland.

http://www.kennedyandboyd.co.uk
admin@kennedyandboyd.co.uk

First published in 2023
Copyright © Duncan Carmichael 2023
Cover design © Zeticula Ltd 2023

Photographs copyright © as credited

Every effort has been made to trace copyright holders of images. Any omissions will be corrected in future editions.

**Hardback ISBN 978-1-84921-238-0**
Paperback ISBN 978-1-84921-237-3

# Contents

# Illustrations

# Introduction

Old Lady Somerset is a fiercely stubborn old bird. In her lifetime she has successfully resisted five attempts at eviction. Within living memory there are two aborted attempts to relocate to Heathfield. Outwith living memory there are failed attempts to move to Carrick Street Oval (1894) and Dam Park (1914 and again in 1919). The lessons of history have been learned. It is not required to have the gift of prophecy to know that there will be no further attempts to remove her from her residence in Hawkhill. She is not a tolerant host. A marked characteristic is a tendency to be kind to her own but inhospitable to visitors. On 29th January, 2019, John Robertson, in his capacity of Inverness Caledonian Thistle manager, made the following comment during a post match press conference: "You know if you lose a goal here the atmosphere can change." Countless other opponents, whether managers, players or supporters, could no doubt give similar testimony to the traditionally raucous atmosphere within the ground. Referees too – although it will be left to your own judgement as to whether they should be labelled as opponents.

This book is not about football *per se*. It is a study of Somerset Park, detailing modifications great and small. Old Lady Somerset is not averse to enjoying a spin. The original playing pitch has twice been spun by 45°. Within these pages the text is punctuated by contemporary maps in order to convey the full impact. Ground rotation may be categorised as major change but ample credence has been afforded to modifications which, although more minor, are nonetheless considered to be significant.

It fires the imagination to think of the original stand being dismantled at Beresford Park then conveyed in a series of horse-drawn carts, down the High Street and over to Hawkhill to be reassembled. However It would be wise not to give away any more spoilers at this stage lest it detracts from the suspense of wondering what happened next. It is misconceived that Somerset Park was named after Somerset Road. The mystery behind the name will be explained but, to repeat the point, the temptation to disclose too much on this page will be resisted.

Our famous old ground is loved not only by home supporters. Polls set up to ascertain Scottish football's favourite away days can always be relied upon to return a swathe of responses in favour of Somerset Park. Yes it is true. Old Lady Somerset is greatly respected, although sometimes feared, by our adversaries.

It was indeed a bygone age when there were no turnstiles at the ground. In those earliest years a tin plate would sit on a table under the surveillance of two or three men. Admission money was thrown onto the plate in the style of a kirk collection. Our forefathers would be incredulous at the thought of paying for admission by tapping on a mobile phone. That is merely one example of progress and it alludes neatly to the crux of this book – progress.

In the summer of 2022 a radical plan for renovation of the north terrace got announced. Consequently Ayr United's managing director, Graeme Mathie, was prompted to mention that this was most important in the evolution of Somerset Park. This planted the seed of an idea from which this book has now grown.

### THE AYR UNITED FAMILY TREE

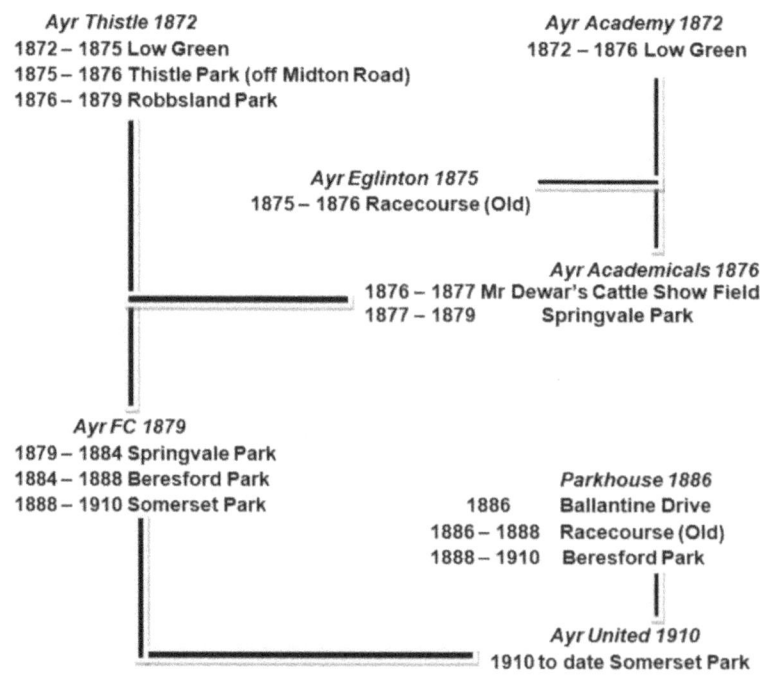

Ayr Thistle 1872
1872 – 1875 Low Green
1875 – 1876 Thistle Park (off Midton Road)
1876 – 1879 Robbsland Park

Ayr Academy 1872
1872 – 1876 Low Green

Ayr Eglinton 1875
1875 – 1876 Racecourse (Old)

Ayr Academicals 1876
1876 – 1877 Mr Dewar's Cattle Show Field
1877 – 1879    Springvale Park

Ayr FC 1879
1879 – 1884 Springvale Park
1884 – 1888 Beresford Park
1888 – 1910 Somerset Park

Parkhouse 1886
1886    Ballantine Drive
1886 – 1888    Racecourse (Old)
1888 – 1910    Beresford Park

Ayr United 1910
1910 to date Somerset Park

*Chapter One*

# Removal from Beresford Park

It may seem a bit of an oddity that Somerset Park dates to 1888 yet Ayr United Football Club originated in 1910. Therein lies a story originating in 1872. The confusion is easily explained, albeit that the explanation requires some intricate, but interesting, detail.

*The steps at the foot of Wellington Lane. Senior football in Ayr evolved from discussions at this spot in 1872.*

The year 1872 was most significant for football. It saw the first FA Cup final and the first international match, Scotland versus England. Viewing it on a more parochial level it was also the year in which Ayr's first football club was formed. It began with a group of youngsters who used to meet at the stairwell at the foot of Wellington Lane. One day their conversation got round to forming a football club. The plan materialised and they called the club Ayr Thistle. No debate was required regarding a suitable field. The vast expanse of the Low Green was yawning in front of them. One of those youths was Thomas Templeton, a future Provost of the town. He was an active participant in the development of football in Ayr, culminating in 1910 when he was a participant in the amalgamation talks between Parkhouse and Ayr FC. Thereafter he was a regular supporter of the newly-formed Ayr United right up until an illness preceded his death at the age of sixty-three in August 1918.

The pitch laid out on the Low Green did not boast billiard table flatness and there were eccentricities in the markings. Compounding the rudimentary nature of the layout were goalposts bereft of nets and with a tape as a crossbar. The pitch ran on an east-west axis. This is known from early reports which referred to "the seaward goal". From a modern day perspective it would be easy to scorn such a set-up. Back then it was conventional and we can be grateful for the chain of events which evolved towards the Somerset Park of today. Where we are today really did begin on the Wellington Lane steps. Ingloriously these steps are now weather beaten and marked by seagull droppings.

In 1875 Ayr Thistle moved to a ground which, in comparison to the Low Green, was always going to be more compact and therefore eminently more suitable. They called it Thistle Park and it was situated just off Midton Road. One year later the club decamped to a ground located at the present day site of Robsland Avenue, off St.Leonards Road. They called it Robbsland (sic) Park. On 22nd April, 1878, Nottingham Forest became the first English club to visit Ayr when they beat Ayr Thistle 3-0 at that ground.

Conditions were considerably less rudimentary when Nottingham Forest next played at Ayr, not least that Victorian football's standard 2:2:6 formation had long since been consigned to history. On that occasion the result was Ayr United 0 Nottingham Forest 2 in an Anglo Scottish Cup tie. That was on 3rd November, 1976 AD (as distinct from the original visit which was BC - Before Clough!).

*Note Robsland Avenue with a single 'b'. It was so named in 1907. The football ground that had formerly occupied this site was known as Robbsland Park. It transpired that the football pioneers were correct with their double 'b' spelling. An Ordnance Survey map dated 1856 shows that the large house at this location was called Robbsland.*

*Robsland Avenue in 2023. It requires a stretch of the imagination to picture Nottingham Forest playing at this location in 1878.*

Elsewhere in the town other developments had been taking place which, in retrospect, were relevant in the context of the Ayr United family tree and the eventual progression towards Somerset Park. Ayr Academy, notwithstanding that school's rugby tradition, adopted the association code in 1872, i.e. they established a football team following on from the formation of Ayr Thistle in the same year. From then until 1876 they played on the Low Green. Ayr Eglinton got formed in 1875 and they played on what we now know as the Old Racecourse but, at that time, the prefix 'Old' did not apply. In 1876 Ayr Academy amalgamated with Ayr Eglinton, the new club being named Ayr Academicals. This new combine set up home on Mr Dewar's Cattle Show field. Even in Victorian times this was deemed to be a clumsy moniker and it soon got renamed Springvale Park. Today the site is marked by that street name, Springvale Park being located off Midton Road.

*Today it is known as the Old Racecourse but when football was played here in the pioneering years the prefix 'Old' was not required.*

*Original Springvale Park street furniture.*

In 1879 Ayr Thistle merged with Ayr Academicals, the new club being called the Ayr Football Club. Springvale Park was the favoured option in the question of venue. It remained the home of Ayr FC until 1884. The name of Ayr Academicals was not lost to history. In September 1884 another club bearing that name got formed.

*Construction of the houses at Springvale Park got underway in 1923 which was forty years after Aston Villa had played on this site. This is the scene in 2023.*

Springvale Park was a superior venue in its day. On 7th November, 1878, it hosted the town's first floodlit match. The teams were Ayr Academicals and Glasgow University. At the far end of the field was a great central light equal to 6,000 candles. At the Midton Road end were two lesser lights, one in each corner. Each lantern was perched on a crudely constructed tower about twenty feet in height. Shortly after half-time the rain increased in intensity thereby making the engine belts slip. In turn the current of the electricity got broken and one after the other the lights went out. In perfect darkness it was abandoned with Glasgow University leading 3-1.

Each year, in June, Springvale Park hosted an athletics meeting, one of the features of which was cycle racing on penny-farthings. The ground earned further distinction when Aston Villa visited on the evening of 26th March, 1883. The eminent visitors beat Ayr FC 5-1 after leading 5-0 at half-time. In December 1922 news emerged that Springvale Park was going to have houses built on it. For most of the previous four decades it had been used for grazing purposes.

On the evening of 14th May, 1884, the Ayr FC Annual General Meeting was held in the Buck's Head, a hostelry which looked down the High Street from the fork in the road where the foot of Alloway Street meets the foot of Kyle Street. It was reported that the club was "in a fairly prosperous position financially." With the bulk of the matches comprising friendlies (in name at least!) the onus was on attracting the type of quality opposition that would get the public rolling in. At Springvale Park they would put their threepence onto a tin plate under the watchful eye of a deputation of committee men. When Queen's Park and Aston Villa visited they had to pay sixpence and for the floodlit match back in 1878 it was an entire shilling. In hindsight there was no apparent motivation for Ayr FC quitting Springvale Park. Speculatively, in the absence of documentary evidence, it may be suggested that the removal to Beresford Park was prompted by the closer proximity to Ayr Station, albeit that it was only several hundred yards closer. The convenience for travelling teams could have been interpreted as a piece of bait to attract illustrious clubs for challenge matches. Springvale Park, though relatively close to the station, still required visiting clubs to hire a horse-drawn conveyance to transport the kit to the ground. In comparison it was an extremely short walk from the station to Beresford Park and the hampers could be carried. The field ran parallel to Beresford Terrace and the site was adjacent to what we now know as Burns Statue Square but it should be pointed out that the statue did not exist in 1884. It got unveiled in July 1891 and, whether by accident or design (probably the former), Rabbie faced right into the football field!

*Ayr FC 1885 with the Ayr and Kilmarnock Charity Cups.*

On Saturday, 23rd August, 1884, Ayr FC hosted Kilmarnock Athletic in the first ever football match played at Beresford Park. Nine weeks later came the ground's first recorded incident of disorder. On that occasion Kilmarnock Athletic were also the visitors but this time it was a third round Scottish Cup tie. Ayr FC won 4-2 but that was not enough to soothe the passions of enraged locals who were most hostile in expressing their disgust at the rough play being meted out. When, for the third time in the match, an Ayr player got laid prostrate, someone broke through the ropes to mete justice on the offender. He was only prevented from doing so by the intervention of the police but the *Ayr Observer* reporter went so far as to comment that, "had the attacker not been prevented, the assault on the player would have been justified". Herein we have mention of another rudimentary aspect of football's pioneering years. That is to say that the playing surface and the spectating areas were divided merely by ropes. A good gate would draw the comment that the ropes were well lined. The converse would cause the reporter to write that the ropes were sparsely lined.

The inaugural Beresford Park season was a successful one. On 30th May, 1885, Ayr FC beat Kilmarnock 3-2 at Rugby Park in the final of the Kilmarnock Charity Cup. It was the first cup the club had ever won. The wait for the club to acquire another trophy was precisely one week. In the inaugural final of the Ayr Charity Cup Kilmarnock were beaten 5-2 at Beresford Park.

Aston Villa agreed to play Ayr FC at Beresford Park on 31st December, 1887. This particular development would prove to be of some relevance in the matter of the club's eventual decision to quit the ground. Aston Villa were holders of the FA Cup having beaten West Bromwich Albion in the 1887 final. Oddly enough they beat Rangers at Crewe in the semi-final (yes it was the FA Cup!). Three weeks after their defeat at Crewe, Rangers were beaten 2-1 by Ayr FC at Beresford Park. The prospective visit of Aston Villa had further interest through the fact that their captain was Archie Hunter, a native of Ayr. He scored in the 2-0 FA Cup final win quite apart from being the winning captain. Hunter had been a full-back for Ayr Thistle in the Robbsland Park days and he appeared for that club when they reached the Scottish Cup semi-finals in season 1876/77 (they lost 9-0 to Vale of Leven). He also played and scored in Aston Villa's win at Springvale Park in 1883. Alas an 1887 Hogmanay homecoming did not happen for Hunter. Preparations for a daunting FA Cup tie against Preston North End on 7th January justifiably got a higher priority. A telegram to confirm Aston Villa's non appearance was tempered by an assurance that they would visit Ayr "at some other time." Consequent to this a tentative arrangement was made for May.

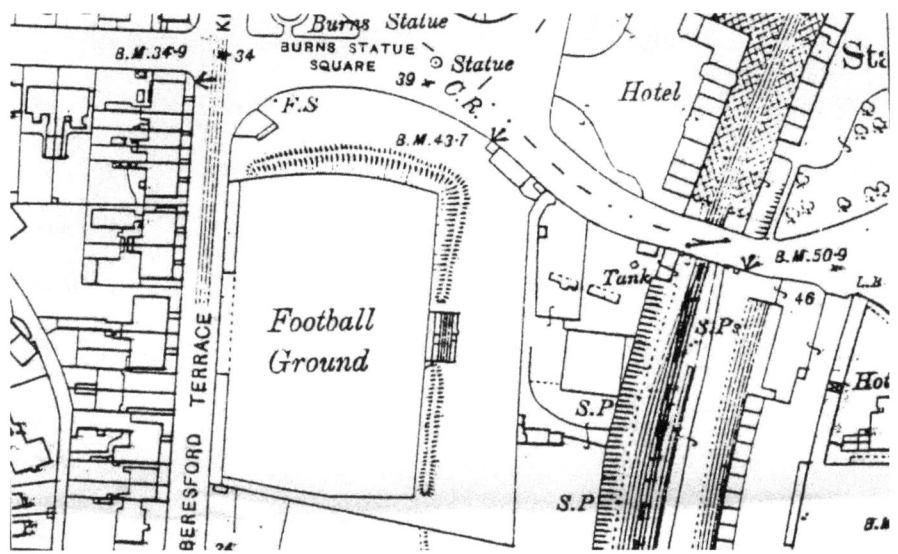

*Beresford Park in its Townhead location.*

The non appearance of Aston Villa may have been a relief to the Ayr FC treasurer. Even with a sixpenny gate any profit would have been minimal and there existed the possibility of a financial loss. The £30 guarantee was not the complete issue and neither was the stipulation to stand a dinner for both teams. Most unreasonably Aston Villa made it a condition that sixty others were to be treated to dinner. At short notice it was not possible to fix up another opponent so, on that last Saturday of 1887, Beresford Park hosted a match between Ayr FC and Ayr Strollers. This was the first team versus the reserve team. The reserves won 4-0. This added credence to the speculation that the first team had consistently been purposely weak in order to give the reserves a better chance of winning the Scottish 2nd XI Cup. Perhaps not surprisingly, just four weeks after beating the supposed first team, they did win the Scottish 2nd XI Cup by beating Hearts reserves 3-1 in an Easter Road final. A fortnight prior to this Ayr FC had beaten Sunderland 4-1 at Beresford Park. By 1895 Sunderland would be the champions of England on three occasions.

With the close of the season within sight Ayr FC's concluding fixture list looked like this.

7th April – Hurlford (home)
14th April – Dumbarton Athletic (home).
21st April – St.Mirren (away)
12th May – Renfrew (away).

After the match on 14th April, the ground would need to be relinquished in order that preparations could be made for the Annual Cattle Show. It was expected, but remained to be confirmed, that Aston Villa would visit on Saturday 5th May by which time the club would be back playing at Beresford Park. The away games were neatly scheduled for the period of time the ground would be unavailable. At least that was the idea. The club anticipated the period of unavailability based on past experience. It seemed reasonable to assume that the Ayrshire Agricultural Association would exercise their right to commandeer Beresford Park using the same period of notice as they had done in 1885, 1886 and 1887. The show was to be spread across Tuesday, 17th April, and Wednesday, 18th April. After playing Dumbarton Athletic on the preceding Saturday it would just be a matter of clearing off for the duration. Although the ground was rented, the grandstand belonged to the club. Inconveniently it had to be dismantled prior to the Cattle Show and re-erected when the club moved back in. In 1888 fate was to dictate that it would be re-erected on a different site.

On Friday, 6th April, the *Ayr Observer* landed in the shops and amongst the tightly packed columns was the unremarkable news that: "Hurlford are expected on Saturday first and Dumbarton Athletic the following Saturday. After that the ground will be required for the Show." Yet between the paper going to press and the Saturday there was a totally unexpected occurrence which was explained in their edition of the following Tuesday (page after page of tightly packed print and they managed to churn it out twice a week!).

"Owing to arrangements required to be made for the Show, Beresford Park was unexpectedly taken early this year and Ayr were unable to play off their fixture with Hurlford. According to former years there should have been play on it for both last Saturday and Saturday coming. To lose the field for a whole month at this time is bound to tell seriously on the funds unless some good half-gates are secured elsewhere. Certainly the men must be kept in practice if they wish to make a respectable show against Aston Villa on Monday, 7th May. Could some other field be obtained? I understand Springvale Park is closed against football."

At least the Aston Villa game was confirmed, albeit for the Monday rather than the anticipated Saturday. On the eve of the Hurlford match the Ayrshire Agricultural Association had carried out a summary requisition of the field in total disregard for the game planned there for the next day, far less the one scheduled there the next week. The last match there prior to the premature eviction had occurred the Saturday before and it had set what was then a record attendance for a game in Ayr. That was the Ayr Charity Cup final with a lamentable result of Ayr FC 1 Kilmarnock 5. At extremely short notice it was agreed to play Hurlford on their own ground. The match was lost 6-4 but it was tellingly observed that: "Some of the Ayr team failed to turn up and did not indicate to the committee their inability to get away. It looks as if winning a badge (although only a silver one) had turned their heads. The Dumbarton Athletic match, scheduled for the next again Saturday, also fell into disarray. That void was filled with an away match against Irvine". (Not to be confused with the not-yet-founded Irvine Meadow). The result, Irvine 2 Ayr FC 1, got blamed on "want of practice." This clearly alluded to Beresford Park not even being available as a training facility.

*The site of the olden day Beresford Park in 2023. In tribute to the club that played here from 1888 to 1910 the street is called Parkhouse Street.*

It all invited the question as to why the ground was taken over prematurely. Surely two additional weeks were not required in order to prepare the venue for the Cattle Show. It was a timescale with no precedent. Yet on taking an objective view the organisers did have justification, although this could not excuse the lack of notice. Why was 1888 different from 1885, 1886 and 1887? You will now be told why. The entries for the event were far in excess of anything the organisers had handled before. It had grown into what was indisputably the largest and most important Cattle Show in Scotland. Prizes in the multitude of categories were substantial. Moreover there was more to it than an exhibition of livestock. A washing machine manufacturer had even booked a stand but we can be assured that an 1888 washing machine would have required a degree of muscle to operate. To couch it in concise terms the unprecedented scale of the event meant that it could no longer be laid out within a few days.

The *Ayr Observer* dated Friday, 13th April, 1888, carried a front page advert which could easily have been missed. It had the proportions of a pin prick amidst the mass of other adverts. The heading on it was Ayr Football Club and it intimated a meeting to be held on Wednesday, 18th April, at 8pm in Carrick Street Hall. There was no ambiguity about the purpose of the meeting. "Business – Ground". Formally it was rounded off with: "By Order of Committee. Jas. Glendinning, Hon. Sec."

The meeting date coincided with the final day of the Cattle Show. It could have been argued that the gathering was therefore pointless. Yet the crux of the matter was the potential for the problem recurring in future years. On that point it was resolved by a majority to quit Beresford Park "on account of the field being so long unoccupied during the preparations for the Cattle Show." The vote to leave was carried by twenty-nine votes to seventeen. By forty-one votes to two it was agreed to move right away. There had been speculation in the early months of 1888 that Ayr Cattle Market would be removed from Killoch Place (a continuation of Beresford Terrace) to the Glebe district of Newton. Had the relocation taken place it is a possibility that future Cattle Shows might have been staged in Newton. Yet this argument was rendered futile by the slim possibility that the move across town would occur. A contemporary report stated: "Ayr must have a Cattle Market, centrally situated, near the railway, large enough for an extending traffic and suitable generally for farmers." Within the year plans did get agreed to move the Cattle Market. The move materialised but the new site, at the foot of Castlehill Road, was still close to Beresford Park. There was no particular requirement for the Cattle Show venue to be close to the Cattle Market site but it had ever been thus. The problem foisted upon Ayr FC had the prospect of remaining for as long as the club continued to inhabit Beresford Park. A secondary factor was that the rent was quite steep due to the Townhead location.

At the Carrick Street Hall meeting it was agreed that the Managing Committee would be delegated the responsibility of finding a new field. Obtaining a suitable field on the town side of the river was considered too daunting a task and this railed against the mindset of a faction of the club's followers who had a prejudice against decamping to the north of the town. Undaunted, the focus then landed on Newton. A betting man would have put money on Newton Park being chosen. It was huge, even encompassing the site on which Newton Park school had yet to be built. In 1888 a journalist saw fit to commend Newton Park for its shrubs and trees but this was tempered by the writer's opinion that the gravel paths were "a little untidy." It was also considered that "the beautiful ornamental seats need a little touching up" and that the 'Keep Off the Grass' signs were not required. The coup de grace was a comment chastising the public for using the park as a free coup. On weighing the demerits against the merits it was discarded as an option but the search remained in that locality.

On 21st April the team journeyed to play St.Mirren at their Westmarch ground. The match formed part of the programme for the St.Mirren FC Sports. Two half-hours were played and it resulted in a 4-1 defeat. A week later, and a fortnight earlier than originally scheduled, a 2-2 draw was contested away to Renfrew. On the eve of playing Renfrew news emerged that the club had been successful in obtaining a new field. The choice came as a surprise for most and a total shock for some.

In the lands of Hawkhill lay an expanse of land adjoining the junction of the Glasgow and Mauchline railway lines. Between the railway and what we now know as Somerset Road, lay three fields (hence the derivation of Tryfield Road a couple of years later, subsequently renamed Tryfield Place). The chosen field was the one closest to the railway line. A lack of grazing meant that the grass was in poor condition. It looked soft and gave the impression that it would be difficult to play on. More positively the turf was old and it was liable to stand a lot of wear. Comparatively the field was short, being just one yard over the minimum designated length. This rendered it seven yards shorter than Beresford Park but at least it was devoid of that ground's slope. However despite the length restrictions it was six yards broader and less crooked. The dismantled club house and stand got carted (literally) to the new site via the High Street. Both structures were re-erected with all haste, each backing onto the railway. On 18th January, 1924, a reunion of Ayr FC players and members was held in Goudie's Restaurant which was situated in the High Street. Walter Lindsay, who had been a committee member, mentioned in his speech that initially they quite simply did not know how they were going to get these structures moved. He recalled similar difficulty in 1884 when the club house had to be shifted from Springvale Park to Beresford Park. Shifting that same club house to Hawkhill was even more taxing and the issue was heavily compounded by having an additional structure to transport this time, the stand. Walter Lindsay explained that, for each of the moves, they put their shoulders to the wheel. Was he talking literally or metaphorically? Probably both!

The pitch ran on a north-south axis and when it was roped off it became apparent that the space was quite restrictive between the ropes and the scanty fence. This land belonged to W.G. Walker & Sons who operated the chemical works on the neighbouring site. In the absence of agreeing a satisfactory rent the whole plan would have foundered but negotiations were swift and mutually agreeable. Walker's also owned the two adjoining fields. In the fullness of time this additional land was to prove crucial to future ground developments.

Somerset Park was chosen as the name. It was an obscure choice. At this time the street currently known as Somerset Road was actually the southern section of West Sanquhar Road. Circa 1908 the residents petitioned the council to rename their section of West Sanquhar Road to Somerset Park Road. By 1909, by way of compromise, it was renamed Somerset Road. So where was the 'Somerset' connotation in 1888? In his excellent book *The Street Names of Ayr*, Rob Close clarified that there was a Somerset Place nearby (now part of Hawkhill Avenue).

Contenders for a ground name could have been Hawkhill Park or West Sanquhar Park yet Somerset Park was agreed upon despite it alluding to a seemingly unobtrusive street. It is sometimes misconceived that Somerset Park was named after Somerset Road but, in truth, it was the other way round.

*Entering Ballantine Drive from the town end today the first house in the street is still called Park House. The name of the football club derived from the house.*

*Parkhouse became a Scottish League club in 1903 but their humble roots were on this piece of land in Ballantine Drive in 1886.*

The creation of Somerset Park caused a bitter division. Straight away letters of resignation were sent by committee members, these rebels even having discussions about forming a rival club. There were forecasts of bankruptcy and rumours quickly spread that the field was in a far worse state than it actually was. "The club will go to the dogs." "The gates will never be as big as they were at Beresford Park." These dissenters took no cognisance of the fact that the majority of the spectators who attended Beresford Park were from the north side of the river. This point was seized upon by the scribe who wrote: "People on the Ayr side of the river cannot grumble very much at the change of ground. Newton folks have trudged to Robbsland, Springvale and Beresford Parks in turn. They deserve to have the matches nearer their homes for a time." It was a fair comment. Newton and Wallacetown were expanding districts as were the nearby villages of Whitletts and Prestwick. Hawkhill was a good catchment area.

It was hoped that Somerset Park would open on Saturday 5th May. Aston Villa having already deferred their visit to Monday 7th May, telegrams were sent to Port Glasgow Athletic and Kilmarnock both of whom understandably declined at such short notice. These declines for the Saturday were a blessing in disguise. This ensured that the ground would now be hanselled by a giant of the English game. Weeks earlier, on 17th April, the Football League had been founded. William McGregor, a Scottish director of Aston Villa, got the credit for being the founder. Until then the measure of success had been the FA Cup which Aston Villa had won the year before.

On the Saturday Aston Villa lost 3-1 to Rangers then travelled to Ayr by the last train. The party then checked into the Ayr Arms Hotel.

On the heavily anticipated Monday night the crowd got entertained by the Ayr Burgh Band, the most popular piece being 'True, true till death'. When the main event got underway, Ayr captain James Campbell won the toss and chose to set Aston Villa against the strong wind. In choosing ends this forfeited the kick-off in favour of Aston Villa. It is on record that: "Archie set the sphere a-rolling for the Villians (sic)." From this it can be deduced that Ayr native Archie Hunter was the first player to kick a ball in earnest at Somerset Park. The match was won 3-0 with two goals from Alex Campbell and one from Feggans (*Ayr Observer*) or one from Alex Campbell and two from Feggans (*Ayrshire Post*). However it can be stated categorically that Alex Campbell scored the first goal at Somerset Park. On 11th January, 2001, your writer received a phone call from someone of that name. He was looking for information about his great grandfather in response to an Ayr Charity Cup winner's medal dated 1887. On closer scrutiny I was able to inform him that his great grandfather had scored the historic first goal at Somerset Park.

On the Saturday prior, Ayr Cricket Club had played their first ever match at their new ground in Newton Park. It was manna from heaven for local sports' journalists, not least the *Ayr Observer* journalist who wrote: "It seems somewhat strange to chronicle in the same issue the opening of two athletic grounds in the same town, one by the Cricket Club, the other by the Football Club. Both were opened by clubs of eminence, the first-named having the premier club of Scotland, the other the ex-champion club of England." In the cricket match referred to Ayr CC had beaten the eminent Edinburgh-based Grange.

On the occasion of Somerset Park's opening it was reported that a big crowd attended. This was attributed to several reasons. These were curiosity, the attraction of Aston Villa, the attraction of Archie Hunter and, finally, the band. While on this topic there was another relevant observation: "The turnout of the fair sex far surpassed what had been the custom at Beresford Park."

"Somerset Park is the best field in Ayrshire." This was said by McKellar, the Beith goalkeeper, on 25th August, 1888, the date of the opening game of the 1888/89 season. We can only ponder how he had the time to survey his surroundings during the most gruelling of shifts. The result was Ayr FC 16 Beith 0. He conceded twelve in the second half. Beith again lost 16-0 at Somerset Park one year later in a first round Scottish Cup tie (7th September, 1889). The beautiful world of coincidence!

Dismantling and reassembling the stand had consequences which, but for luck, could have proved fatal. During an Ayr Charity Cup final it collapsed. This occurred on 25th May, 1889, while Ayr FC faltered towards a 3-1 defeat against Kilbirnie. One scribe managed to insert a touch of humour into his description of the event. "The collapse of the grand(?) stand was an appropriate climax of the afternoon's misfortune. Those who received slight injury are thankful that they were so little damaged and others are happy at their lucky escape."

There was another occasion when the stand almost came to grief. On 23rd February, 1895, Ayr FC beat Saltcoats Victoria 6-1 in an Ayrshire Combination fixture. A spark from a passing train set fire to the slope behind the stand which was then under threat of burning down along with the barricade behind it. This potentially dire situation was averted by the intervention of some supporters. "The willing hands, or rather, feet of a few bystanders prevented the flames from doing any damage."

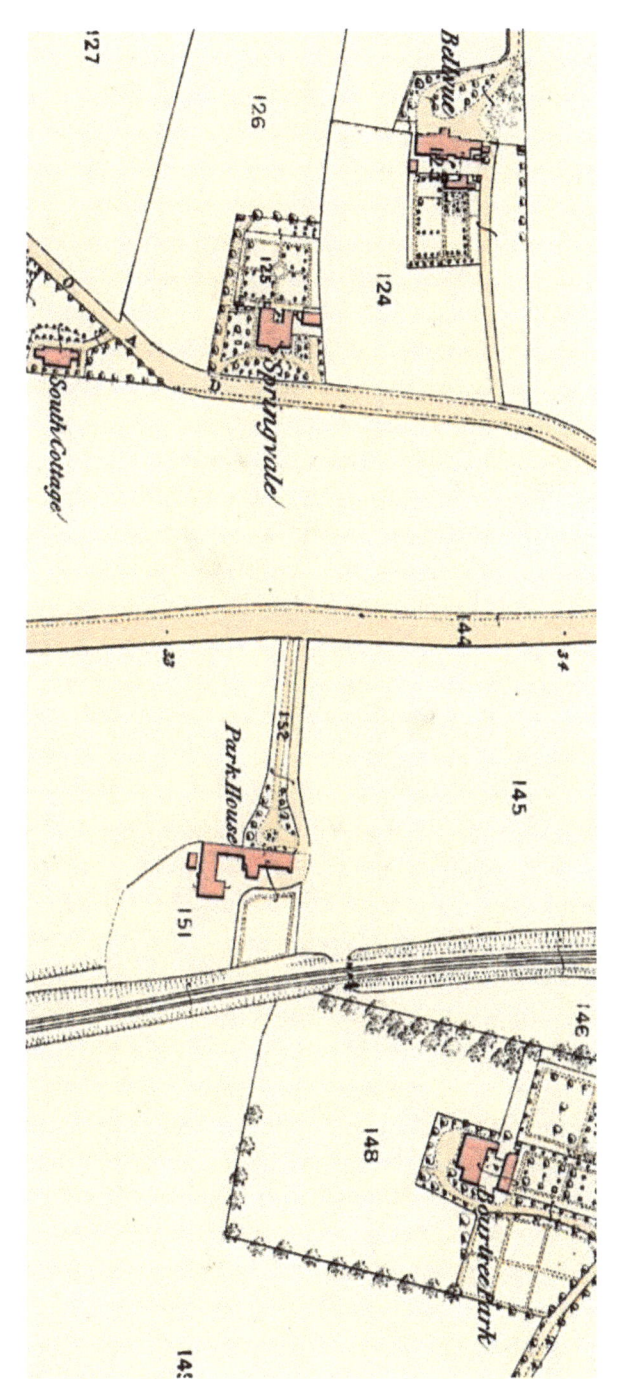

*Prominent on this 1856 Ordnance Survey map are the names Springvale and Park House. In later decades those locations were conspicuous in the evolution of football in Ayr.*

*Chapter Two*

# Greater Somerset

The *Ayr Observer* dated Friday, 13th July, 1894, stated the following in terms which appeared categorical and unambiguous.

"It is now definitely announced that the Ayr club have resolved to take a more central ground and have been very fortunate in securing Carrick Street Oval which has entrances from both Carrick Street and High Street. It is expected that this will draw out a lot of people who have not always had time to visit Somerset Park."

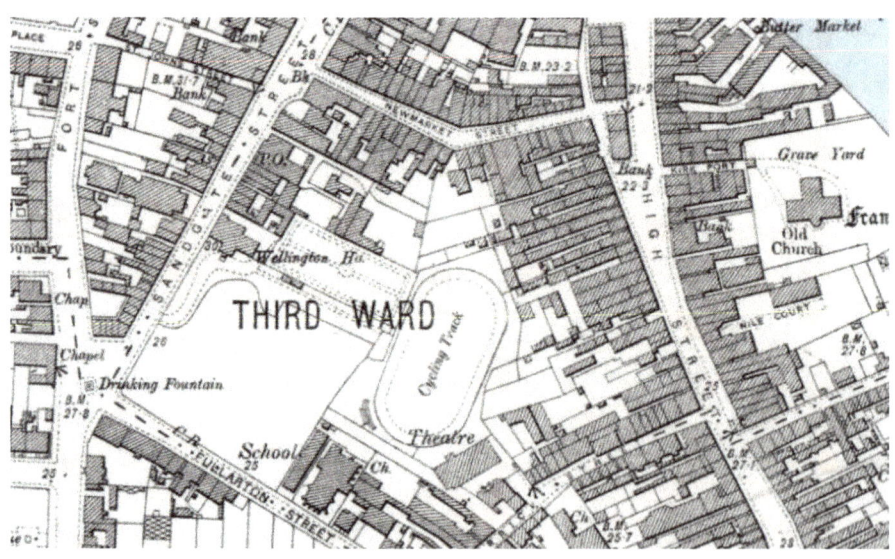

*Map showing the location of Carrick Street Oval.*

The story was not totally wayward but the journalist was premature in assuming that the negotiations would be concluded without a hitch.

By early August agreement was still being sought, at which time the *Ayr Observer's* sports writer was clear in his view: "Unquestionably they are in a remote corner of the globe at present and very ungetable (sic), and football club executives do not study to have their exhibitions 'far from the madding crowd' but prefer an arena where the 'madding crowd' will congregate in countless thousands." Carrick Street Oval had characteristics which were the envy of the Ayr FC committee but had nothing to do with the central location. A clue can be found in the more formal name for that venue. It was the Ayr Cycling and Athletic Grounds. It was a burning desire of Ayr FC to have first class facilities for athletics and cycling. Such facilities were denied by Somerset Park's hemmed-in location. What were the options?

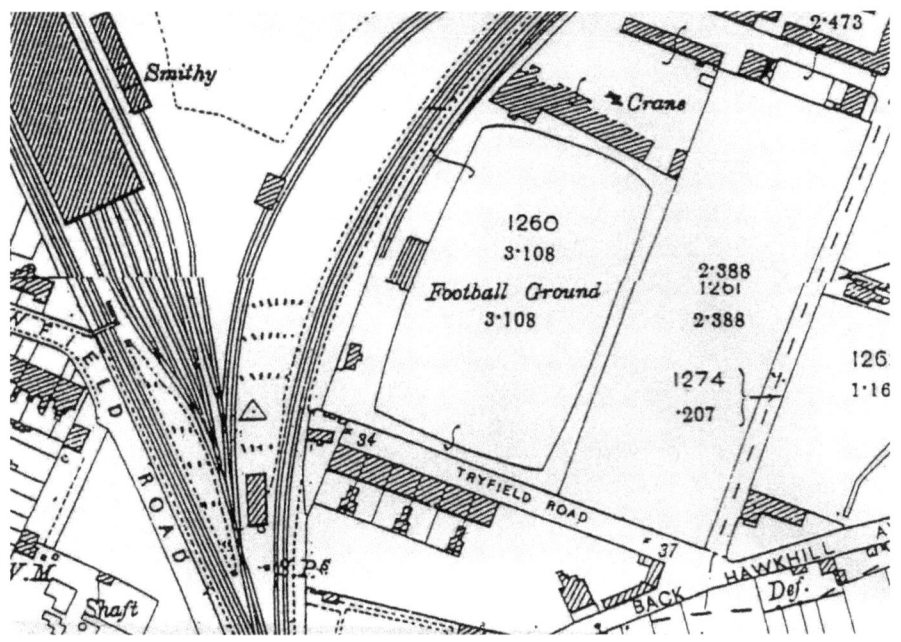

*Alignment of Somerset Park 1888 to 1897.*

On the Fair Saturday in July 1896 the Ayr Amateur Athletic Club held a sports meeting. This was the athletic section of Ayr Football Club. The event was successful, even in view of Somerset Park's restrictions. Emboldened by that success it was proposed to lay a cinder track at the ground. That proposal was soon discarded in favour of far loftier aspirations.

On the evening of 5th August, 1896, a meeting was held to discuss the ongoing issue of athletics facilities. A proposal to rent a field next to Blackhouse (in the vicinity of where Ayr Racecourse now is) had already failed to catch on. Any development would now take place at the existing site. The meeting agreed that a tarmacadam track would be laid down for bicycle and foot runners. Rapid negotiations were carried out with W.G. Walker & Sons who were "very considerate in their terms, both as landlords and in the construction of the track." A very good neighbour! W.G.Walker & Sons had already laid a tarmacadam track at Celtic Park. With the club having failed in its application to join the Second Division of the Scottish League for 1896/97, there existed a hope that the scale of this work would see the next application more favourably considered. A further season in the Ayrshire Combination was a less than challenging prospect, the club having won it every season since it had been formed in 1893. Yet fulfilling the 'track' dream stood to incur a huge cost irrespective of the co-operation from the kindly landlord. The estimated expense was "near on £400". If that figure was frightening the ultimate cost was truly terrifying. It would set the club back nearly £700. Compounding the magnitude of this was the fact that debt already existed before agreeing to the work.

In order to accommodate the expansion it was necessary to intrude on the neighbouring field. No longer would the pitch be running parallel to the railway on a north to south axis. On completion of the work it would be running diagonally on a north-east to south-west axis, at an angle to the railway, with the club house and stand being shifted to the Tryfield Place side of the ground.

On Monday, 8th March, 1897, the work began. This news was heralded with a prophecy that: "The track when finished should equal anything in the provinces." A further prophecy had no hope of being fulfilled. "Somerset Park will be closed for a week or two while the contractor is going on with his work of transforming Somerset into Greater Somerset." After a 2-2 draw in a friendly against Cambuslang on 6th March no football was played at Somerset Park until an Ayrshire Combination fixture against Stevenston Thistle on 17th April. Even at six weeks the timescale was commendable.

By late March news of the development was starting to reach the world at large. There was a report that some of the running and cycling champions would be appearing at the new facility. It was even dared to suggest that potential world champions would appear. This was not necessarily outrageous optimism. Several years later, in the Edwardian era, Dan Flynn was to compete at Somerset Park. He was the greatest Scottish cyclist of his generation.

By the start of April the contractor had commenced to re-lay the turf. This was considered to be the most important priority because the track would not be required for immediate use. Yet the laying of the track fired the public imagination more than any other aspect. While the work steadily progressed the platitudes remained unabated. "The track, when finished, will be one of the best, or the best, in the provinces, and will not be inferior to any track in Scotland, albeit that it may be beaten in length as it will be about a half- lap shorter than the Celtic track. The quality, however, is a particular item of the contract."

On 3rd April, Ayr FC had to forfeit ground advantage in order to fulfil an Ayrshire Combination fixture against Beith. In a 4-3 defeat Jock Millar was sent off. Offsetting this misery was the expectation that Somerset Park would be in playable condition by the next Saturday provided that the weather was favourable. The weather was not inclement enough to prevent completion of the re-turfing operation within that time, albeit that the incomplete track was described as being ragged. However the foundation was not yet strong enough to withstand a ninety-minute test. Fortunately there was a further week's grace because the match on 10th April was scheduled for Beresford Park anyway. That entailed a 2-0 defeat against Parkhouse in the Ayrshire Championship. This competition had little interest yet losing was a blow considering the burning hatred between the clubs. Ayr FC had undergone practically no training during the previous four weeks owing to the ongoing work. The club's gymnasium was located within the club house but, understandably, the place had been in a state of chaos.

Would the ground be in use for the scheduled match with Stevenston Thistle on 17th April? Yes it would. The Ayrshire Combination was another of those competitions which did little to fire the public interest but the big draw was to see the transformation. Incessant rain had the effect of modifying the attendance to "fairly good". The match was hailed as the opening of Greater Somerset. Although the pitch had been re-laid the track was incomplete but at least people were able to imagine what it would look like when finished.

"It would be a bad business to lose in the first game on Greater Somerset. Will the transformation harbour luck?" The *Ayr Observer* correspondent need not have feared. In a move initiated from the kick-off George Ballantyne scored. The first goal at Greater Somerset had taken a matter of seconds to achieve. Winning the match 4-2 drew less conversation than the topic of the surrounds. A contemporary report tells us: "That amazement was rife amongst those round the track was evident from the many flattering criticisms one could hear bestowed on the track, committee and club officials in general." People even went so far as to call it the Celtic Park of Ayrshire. Interest in the project was illustrated by the fact that the Maybole Carrick Cycling Club arranged a spin to Dunure and then on to Ayr where their attention was divided between the match and the partially completed track.

There was also a Victorian manifestation of Cameron's Bar on that day. In celebration of the re-opening, the gymnasium within the club house was requisitioned as a bar. It was staffed by four young women who struggled to cope with the demand. At half-time they were described as "bathed in perspiration." The choice consisted of porter or ales.

No photographs were taken on the day Greater Somerset was opened. Readers will probably be most unsurprised at that. Photography at a football match in 1897? It would not have happened anyway! Or would it? Well, on the previous Saturday, a photographer turned up for the derby against Parkhouse at Beresford Park. Reproducing his photographs in the local newspapers was beyond the technological know how of the day but readers were given the following description.

"The camera was manipulated by Mr Dixon (agent for J. Lizars) Union Buildings. The photos are nicely mounted and are characteristically plain, showing incidents in different stages of the game and at critical moments, the incidents at goal being very striking. Any of these pictures can be had for the sum of sixpence and they can be enlarged if so desired. Football enthusiasts should give Mr Dixon a call and he will, we are told, be only too pleased to give a resumé of the game without the usual din and excitement."

With the equipment available to him Mr Dixon had undoubted skill in being able to get photographs from moving action. In contrast it would have been less taxing to have an inanimate redeveloped Somerset Park as his subject. After his stint the week before he was not minded to turn up for the opening of Greater Somerset. Even if he had the photos would have been long lost anyway. Had it been different it would have been well worth a sixpence! Hence we must be grateful for the old maps. Goalkeeper Archie McDonald would have been an entertaining photographic study. He played with a blackened face in this historic match. Such were the rigours of playing football after a shift at work and no workplace washing facilities. It was not an unusual sight to see players taking the field with blackened knees.

Developments elsewhere in 1897 vindicated the move to Hawkhill. In that year Victoria Bridge was constructed as well as Northfield Avenue. Bit by bit the district was becoming more accessible. That year also saw the construction of a large tenement building spanning nearby Cross Street (now known as King Street) and Limond's Wynd. The influx of population to the area was growing apace.

The elephant in the room was the substantial debt. Thomas Brown, the treasurer, must have been ill at ease. £10 got paid to the club for allowing Greater Somerset to be used for the Ayrshire Cup final (Kilmarnock Athletic 3 Kilmarnock 0). Then April was concluded with an Ayr Charity Cup tie for which the admission was on the hefty side at sixpence. With a result of Ayr FC 7 Annbank 2 it was good value yet the pricing was in excess of what would have been anticipated for such a game on a Tuesday night. To make more substantial inroads on the huge deficit a priority had to be the means of making money from the track. There was a club rule that the treasurer had to post up his annual report in the club house at least one week before the Annual General Meeting. In 1897 it would have been done in trepidation.

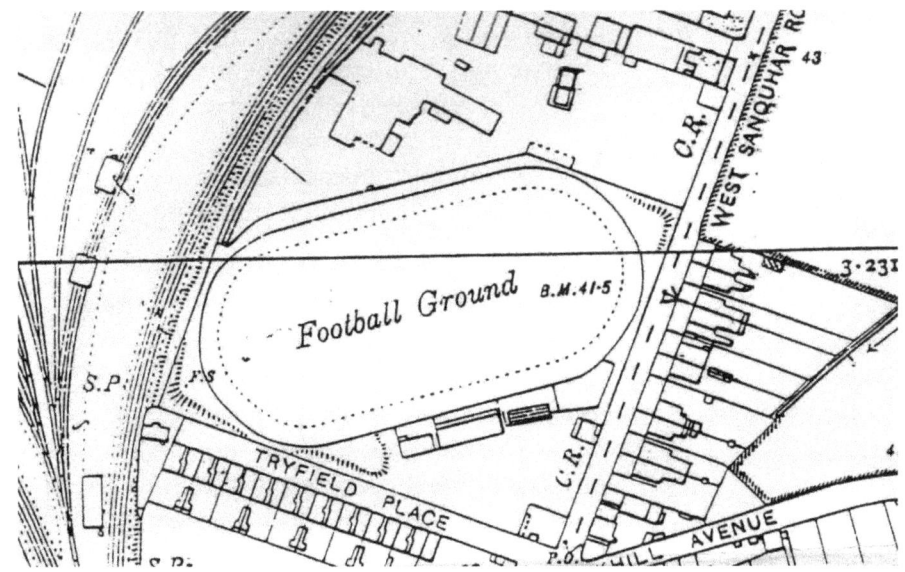

*Alignment of Somerset Park 1897 to 1924.*

On 16th June the track was opened. The occasion was a sports meeting organised by the Ayr Football and Athletic Club. It would be 1899 before the club formally changed name from the Ayr Football Club but the elongated moniker had long since been used by the newspapers. This event took place on a Wednesday evening and attracted a crowd estimated at 2,000. Heavy rain during the day had created fears of a postponement. Although successful to a degree, this was little more than a tester for the main event. That took place on the Saturday afternoon of 17th July with an overspill event on the evening of Monday 19th July. The drawings on the Saturday amounted to £150 from an estimated turnout of 5,000. On the Monday the receipts were less than a third of that yet the signs were encouraging. The track was beginning to yield a handsome return. With the application to join the Second Division of the Scottish League being successful this presented further potential for financial reward.

League football and the continuing success of the annual sports did create increased income yet the task of managing the debt seemed insurmountable. In April 1898 the Annual General Meeting took place in the Masonic Hall in Nile Court. Some debt had been removed but the figure was still £600. The chief business of the meeting was the consideration of a proposal to levy £1 on the club's members in order to address at least some of the deficit. This did not go down well therefore 'compulsion' was modified to 'contributions invited'.

In December 1899 the half-yearly meeting was held in the Newton Council Rooms and the theme was familiar. The secretary's report was described as "discouraging" and the treasurer's report drew a description of "very depressing." It was so bleak that the question of amalgamation with Parkhouse was raised. Desperate though things were there was no support for the idea. A reporter summarised the conclusion in rhyme.

"Each and all took off their several ways,
Hoping and praying for better financial days."


*On 11th June, 1962, a postal package arrived at Somerset Park. It was sent anonymously. The inscription showed that it was an Ayr Cycling Club trophy, shown opposite. Further inscriptions showed the respective winners of a five-mile handicap from 1895 to 1900. Cycling's rise and fall in popularity contributed, in turn, to seismic changes at Somerset Park.*

In February 1901 a plan was put into action with the sole purpose of erasing the debt accrued in 1897. This was a venture advertised as "The First Bazaar of The Century". Since it was now the fourteenth month of the century this claim could have been open to scrutiny. The second day of the event was opened by the distinguished Sir William Arrol MP, of Seafield. He was an eminent engineer who had been involved in the construction of the Forth Bridge and Tower Bridge, both of which are still landmarks of world renown. The bazaar took the form of a mock Japanese village and tea garden. A sum of £325 was taken over the two days which, although significant, was far short of what had been hoped for. The creation of Greater Somerset had come at a price and it was still being paid.

Was there any hope of a rich benefactor? The team played in the Duke of Portland's colours of broad black and white stripes. This was just a coincidence though. The esteemed gent had no connection to Ayr FC. What about the Earl of Eglinton? Didn't he make an appearance at the club's sports meeting in July 1897? He was expected but did not show!

In season 1901/02 the club made a profit of £96 : 17s : 7d. For 1902/03 the profit was £155 : 6s : 4d. The 1903/04 season saw a profit of £413 : 15s : 1d. 1904/05 returned a loss of £300 : 12s : 7d. The club reported that: "The loss during 1904/05 is largely accounted for by the fact of the club being defeated in the second round of the Qualifying Cup competition. The gross drawings from this source in the previous year were £554 and for the year under review £46."

By June 1905 the lease for Somerset Park had just six years to run. It contained a vaguely ominous clause which read: "It is only terminable in special circumstances by the proprietor at a term of Whitsunday after 1907 on giving twelve months notice." This gave rise to the question as to whether it would be advisable to plough funds into enhancing the ground should there be future prosperity. How would the club stand in relation to security of tenure? Today a 99-year lease is not uncommon. Six years with a clause that could be invoked in two years time was a somewhat fragile tenure.

A share issue was floated in order to raise £1,000, these shares comprising 2,000 at ten shillings each. The list opened on 1st September, 1905, and closed on 11th September. The prospectus contained a neat insight of what Somerset Park was like.

*The 1905 share prospectus, opposite, aimed at raising £1,000.*

# The Ayr Football and Athletic Club,

### LIMITED.

# PROSPECTUS.

*Registered Office:*

## SOMERSET PARK, HAWKHILL, AYR.

Printed by Hugh Henry, Newmarket Street, Ayr.

"The ground is situated in one of the most thickly populated districts of the town and is easily accessible by road and rail and is within easy approach of Newton on Ayr Railway Station. The proposed extension of the Corporation Electric Tramways, which will pass close to the ground, will further add to the convenience of approach. The grounds are well banked, and afford the spectators an uninterrupted view of the field of play; while there are two commodious Grand Stands, one of which is covered, with dressing rooms and other accommodation underneath."

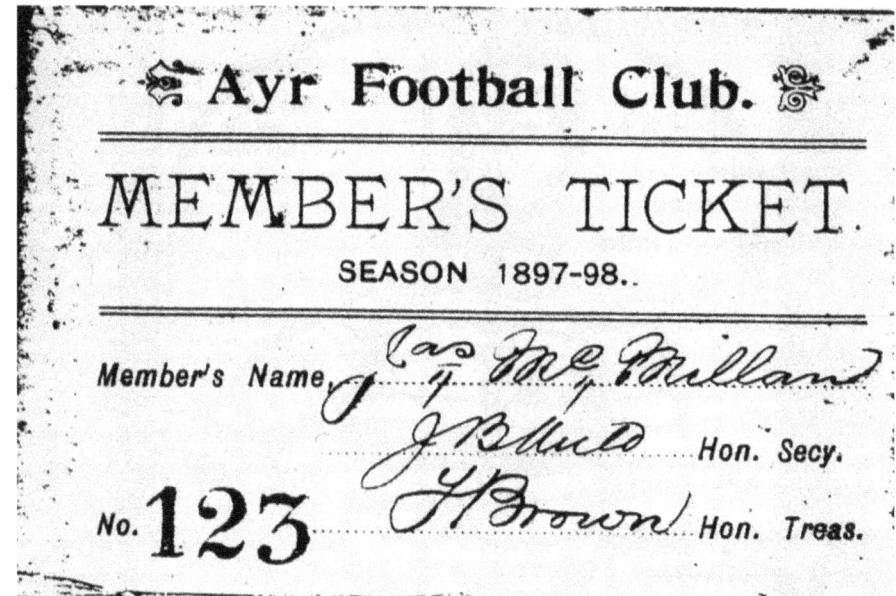

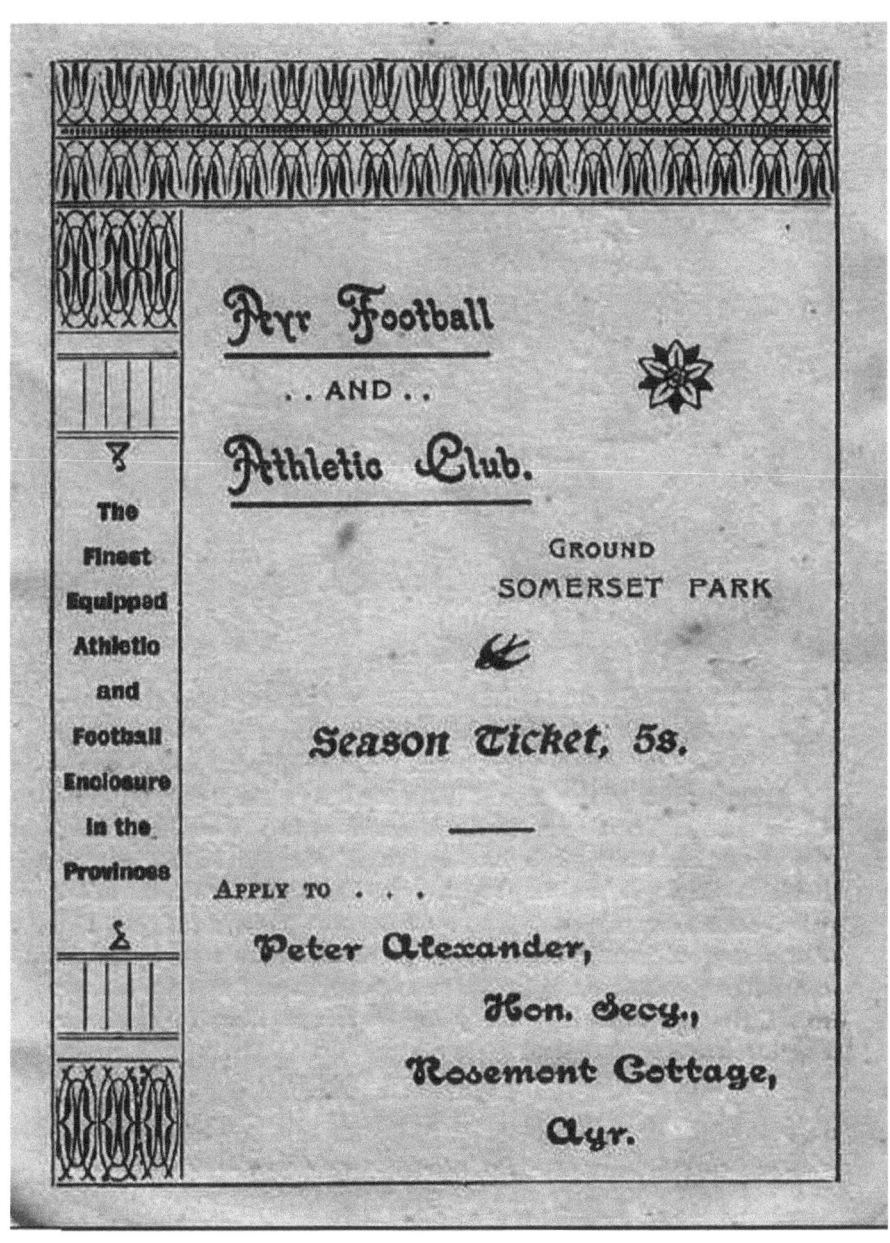

*This advert for season tickets appeared in a booklet produced by Ayr FC in 1901. Note the boastful description of Somerset Park.*

## Chapter Three

# The Grand Plan

As of Monday, 9th May, 1910, Ayr FC no longer existed. On that evening a large attendance turned up at the Masonic Hall in Nile Court for a meeting of the club's shareholders. The subscribers of 1905 now held the power to create Ayr United.  This was the last in a series of meetings and counter meetings relating to a proposed amalgamation with Parkhouse. The mover of the amendment that there be no amalgamation failed to find a seconder. Consequently the motion agreeing to the proposal got carried, Parkhouse having already consented. This remains the only amalgamation of two existing Scottish League clubs. The newly formed Ayr United now had two grounds at its disposal. That other ground was Beresford Park which Parkhouse had moved into shortly after Ayr FC's departure in 1888 having previously played on the Racecourse (Old) and at Ballantine Drive on their formation in 1886. Ayr United's birth arrived during a period of national mourning. King Edward V11 died three days earlier.

The future of Somerset Park and the club in general was initially determined by a committee representing the two dissolved clubs plus three neutral members. This comprised James Lyon (Ayr FC), Archie Buchanan junior (Ayr FC), John Kerr (Ayr FC), Fred Dewar (Ayr FC), ex-Provost Thomas Templeton (Parkhouse), Tom Steen (Parkhouse), J.Kay (Parkhouse), W.Ferguson (Parkhouse), T.C. Dunlop (neutral), W.G. Wallace (neutral) and ex-Provost William Allan (neutral). You may recall the name Thomas Templeton from Chapter One. He was one of the youths who were inspired to form Ayr Thistle back in 1872. Harry Murray (Ayr FC) and Tom Welsh (Parkhouse) became joint secretaries pro tem.

The ease with which the amalgamation was agreed was based on a delusion that Ayr United would immediately gain admittance to the First Division. In support of the application the pro tem secretaries penned a letter which was circulated to member clubs in the hope of gaining enough votes for entry. The failed enterprise left the legacy of an interesting letter that was punctuated with some favourable aspects of Somerset Park which had already been favoured over Beresford Park.

Dear Sirs,

We beg to inform you that an application has been made on behalf of Ayr United Football and Athletic Club for admission to the First Division of the Scottish Football League and, on behalf of the directors of said club, we beg to solicit your support and vote at the Annual General Meeting of the League.

In support of our application we may say that this club is the outcome of an amalgamation of the Ayr and the Ayr Parkhouse Football Clubs, both of which, as you are aware, are, and have been for a number of years, members of the Second Division of the Scottish League. It has been recognised by members of both clubs that, with a divided patronage, and consequent inferior football fare, the town and district of Ayr is not catered for as it deserves. As a sporting centre Ayr is unrivalled, which is evidenced by the support accorded to every branch of sport when served up in first-class quality. The athletic sports and annual races are not surpassed in Scotland and, when the football matches have at all been attractive, the public support has not been withheld.

Each of the clubs now amalgamating has on several occasions drawn from £150 to £200 in football matches and if this could be attained with second class teams and divided public support then we claim to have good grounds for anticipating very much better results with a first class team and patronage. The district is a large and populous one, possessing as it does, a population of at least 90,000 within a fifteen mile radius and there is not the slightest doubt of its ability to successfully support a First League club. Another important factor, and one which should commend itself to your favourable consideration, is the accessibility of Ayr from all quarters. Taking Glasgow as the centre there is an excellent train service with only an hour's journey and this applies not only to access to, but egress from, the town, so that clubs can always rely on being immune from early outward travelling and late return journeys.

The capital of the club has been fixed at £4,000 and (with the exception of about £1,000, which represents the holding of the two clubs and is more than secured by their assets) the whole of this capital will be available for organisation and development. The financial stability of the club is thus assured and this fact of itself is of sufficient importance to justify a preference in our favour.

The ground is within easy distance of the station and the playing pitch is without doubt quite the equal of that of any league club. Its sandy nature and proximity to the seashore keeps it in perfect condition at all times and it is an almost unheard of thing for a game to be postponed in Ayr through the unplayability of the ground. The holding capacity is estimated at 15,000 and this number has several times, on the occasion of the annual sports, been exceeded. There is also ample room for extension.

From the foregoing statement of facts we submit we have reasonable claims for our admission to the First League and respectfully solicit your cordial sympathy and support.

Yours truly

(Signed) T.M. Welsh

                    Joint secretaries pro tem

(Signed) H.Murray

Stating that Somerset Park had several times exceeded crowds of 15,000 was being a bit elastic with the truth, notwithstanding the immense popularity of the annual sports. By starting life in the Second Division the ground capacity would not be tested in the immediate future unless there was a particularly attractive Scottish Cup draw. However even that prospect had a hurdle. Ayr United's position in the hierarchy of Scottish football was such that the club still had to compete in the Scottish Qualifying Cup.

The Annual General Meeting of the Scottish League took place on Tuesday, 7th June, 1910. Two places were available in the First Division because Morton had to undergo re-election and Port Glasgow Athletic had relegated themselves by resigning from that league. The clubs applying were Morton (sixteen votes), Raith Rovers (thirteen votes), Ayr United (two votes), Abercorn (one vote) and Dumbarton (no votes). Leith Athletic, the Second Division champions, did not even apply. Dundee Hibernian (name changed to Dundee United in 1923) got voted into the Second Division to fill the vacancy created by the amalgamation of the Ayr clubs.

In the summer of 1910 Somerset Park remained adequate for the purpose but for how long? On merit Ayr United would have made it into the hallowed sphere of the First Division after one year with the team finishing as runners-up in the Second Division in 1910/11. In a system that was borderline corrupt, merit had no bearing. After winning the title in 1911/12 the Annual General Meeting of the Scottish League took place on 3rd June. A motion was carried to allow the highest club in the Second Division to automatically pass into the First Division only for a quite incredulous u-turn when the St.Mirren delegate complained that

Ayr United's promotion would have caused his club's relegation and he said that this would be unfair because they were already committed to a First Division wage bill.

Ayr United retained the Second Division title in 1912/13 and once more the question of promotion was at the mercy of the vote at the League's Annual General Meeting on 2nd June. The requisite number of votes materialised and the club got promoted along with Dumbarton who had finished sixth. Sixth! It was an appalling set-up further accentuated by the First Division being extended by two clubs to accommodate Ayr United and Dumbarton. God forbid that anyone should be relegated! Since the season's end the talk of promotion had been prolific. On the night of the vote a large crowd gathered outside the Ayrshire and Galloway Hotel despite the rain. Tom Steen was the Ayr United chairman and his family owned the hotel. It was known that a telegram bearing the result would be sent there. The news created great jubilation amongst the rain bedraggled supporters.

*The Somerset Park athletics meeting on 19th July, 1913.*

Would Somerset Park be suitable to host First Division crowds? Earlier in 1913 the ground had been put to the test. On 8th February, First Division Airdrie had visited for a second round Scottish Cup tie. There was no tinge of exaggeration to the observation that: "Enthusiasm in the district has never before been equalled in the history of the game." Special trains were laid on from Airdrie, Dalmellington and Girvan. Local media sources put the crowd at 9,000 and the *Glasgow Herald* estimated it at 11,000. This test to the holding capacity occurred with the club making no extensions or alterations. It was reported that: "The stand could have been filled twice over with the number of people who were turned away after the sitting accommodation had been taken up." By reason of a 2-0 defeat the next test to the holding capacity would be in the First Division.

On the conclusion of the club's fixtures it had been far from guaranteed that the Second Division title would be retained. Abercorn had all of six games left from which they required seven points to win the league. Their lamentable run-in comprised four defeats, a win and a draw, so they finished fourth. Yet even with due allowance for the fact that league positions did not have a complete bearing on promotion there was a confidence that Ayr United's election to the First Division was a likely contingency.

While Abercorn were imploding the club set about implementation of a greater capacity. W.G. Walker & Sons generously granted Ayr United, without increase of rent, an additional piece of ground in order to assist that objective. This additional ground extended the entire length of Somerset Park on the Walker's side and it had a depth of about five yards. The banking operation got underway with no delay thereby increasing the standing capacity by several thousand.

Throughout July 1913 improvements were swiftly made. A press box with a capacity of sixteen got constructed at the end of the stand nearest the railway and a room for the referee and linesmen was made within the gymnasium. The number of turnstiles was increased from nine to fourteen and a gate for boys and cyclists was built in Tryfield Place. By way of a disclaimer it should be clarified that gender specific references are merely a reflection of football at that time.

The first home game in the First Division was a visit from Hearts which attracted a crowd estimated at, or close to, 8,000. Long before kick-off the stand was packed and it need hardly be said that the seats arranged around the track were also filled. Accommodating spectators on trackside seating may seem an alien concept in today's world of safety regulations. However it should be borne in mind that the cycle track allowed for those seats to be placed at a relatively safe distance from the playing action. How would the place cope with an Old Firm visit? Celtic were at Ayr a couple of days after Christmas and the question was not properly answered because gales and drenching showers restricted the attendance to about 5,000.

The Ayr United board believed that Somerset Park was inadequate. W.G. Walker & Sons had always been an extremely co-operative landlord yet the security of tenure could not be taken for granted. Would further investment in the facilities be prudent? The mindset of the directors was made known in early February 1914 when news leaked out that the club was in negotiation with the Ayrshire Agricultural Association for a lengthy lease of Dam Park. In the columns of the *Ayrshire Post* the rationale was succinctly explained. "At present Somerset Park is held on conditions which do not justify the club laying out the money necessary to make the ground and appurtenances on a level with the best enclosures and in addition there is not much room for extension." The obvious advantage of Dam Park was its more central location in addition to which the playing pitch was large and in good order. More debatable was the belief that it could be made to hold 50,000 spectators at very little cost. It stood to reason that the pitch was in good order since the lease was held by Ayr Cricket Club. It was anticipated that Ayr Cricket Club would not place any obstacles in the way if Ayr United were to negotiate satisfactorily with the Ayrshire Agricultural Association. The anticipation was a delusion. With the cricket fraternity still having several years left on their lease the idea was that Ayr United would share Dam Park. It was screamingly obvious that the cricketers would be dead set against this. Their case was set out in the following terms.

"Since entering upon the tenancy of Dam Park the club have nursed that ground with the greatest care and the result has been the making of pitches which would be hard to beat anywhere in Scotland. Certain members of the management have spared neither time nor money in their endeavours to make the ground as perfect as possible. Can football be played on a cricket pitch without to a certain extent damaging it and making it less suitable to the summer game? A number of the cricketers say that it cannot. If Ayr United are successful in their application it will mean that it will not be possible to keep the cricket pitch in a condition satisfactory to the wants of a club of the standing of Ayr Cricket Club."

There was a certain amount of naivety in the initial assumption that the cricketers would consent to professional football being played on their pitch. The Ayrshire Agricultural Association ultimately rejected Ayr United's misguided initiative.

With the intervention of the Great War thoughts of redeveloping or relocating were understandably forgotten for the duration. In 1919, by which time the hostilities were over, the Ayr United directorate revived the notion of moving. Attempts to abandon Old Lady Somerset had failed in 1894 and 1914. Where was the proposed new location in 1919? It was Dam Park again. On Tuesday, 17th June, the matter came before a meeting of the Ayrshire Agricultural Association. The lease had expired a year earlier but, with the war still in progress, the matter had been left in abeyance. Now there were rival claims from Ayr Cricket Club and Ayr United. Having held the lease for so long it was natural that the cricketers did not wish to relinquish their pitch. With Mr J.H.Turner of Cessnock Castle presiding, the rival claims were urged with great eloquence. By a substantial majority it was agreed to renew the lease in favour of Ayr Cricket Club. Dam Park could be forgotten for now but only until 1972. Of course Beresford Park was also at the club's disposal. Ayr United reserves played there. That option was not remotely considered as a new base. It met favour with the tired old argument about having a central location but this was negated by the fragile tenure. In time the fear of Beresford Park not having security of tenure would be validated. In May 1926 the owners, the London Midland and Scottish Railway Company, terminated Ayr United's lease. The motive was that they wished to use it for recreational purposes for railway employees. In consequence it could no longer be used for reserve fixtures.

The jewel in the crown of the 1897 development was the tarmacadam cycle track but by 1919 there had been a shift in sporting tastes. On Saturday, 19th July, and Monday, 21st July, the annual sports were held at Somerset Park. Not more than 6,000 attended the Saturday event, a figure several thousand below pre-war gatherings. No blame could be attached to the industrious organisers. A decline in the popularity of watching cycling was the crucial factor. This contributed to a dilemma which hinged on three facts. 1. The club was forced to remain at Somerset Park. 2. The cycle track was a white elephant. 3. Albeit that the landlord had always been most accommodating, the possibility of the lease being invoked remained a nagging worry.

By December 1919 the directors were perusing the notion of offering to buy Somerset Park but cautiously it was thought wise to assess the potential of the ground first. In that month Archibald Leitch was called in. He was an expert planner of football grounds. It was a sign of ambition that someone of such eminence was consulted. By mid-January 1920 the decision to buy the ground was pressed ahead with. W.G. Walker & Sons, ever amenable in assisting Ayr United, once more displayed kind co-operation. After smooth negotiations it was agreed that the purchase price would be £2,500 comprising five annual payments of £500, each payable on Whitsunday (the seventh Sunday after Easter). On 11th June, 1920, the first instalment got paid, albeit several weeks after the Whitsunday deadline. With interest it amounted to £536 : 10s : 6d.

*The first instalment for the purchase of Somerset Park on 11th June, 1920. £536 :10s : 6d including interest.*

It was quite extraordinary that within several months of agreeing to the transaction, Ayr United accumulated a windfall greater than the entire amount required for the complete purchase. Johnny Crosbie was a natural footballer who possessed great ball skills. He had been signed from Muirkirk Athletic on 6th October, 1913. In April 1920 he was placed on the transfer list at his own request. He had ambitions to quit his native Glenbuck to further his football career. Almost right away there was interest from Sheffield Wednesday, Burnley and Newcastle United. The first bid came from Newcastle United and it was £2,500. However this was outmatched by Birmingham City and on the Wednesday afternoon of 5th May, 1920, a delegate from that club got Johnny's signature. Based on the failed Newcastle United bid speculation put the transfer fee at £3,000. In truth Ayr United received £2,800 plus a further sum of £54 : 5s : 3d in interest due to payment not being made until March 1921. The sale of one player therefore more than covered the purchase of Somerset Park. In September 1979, by which time he was living in Ayr, Johnny Crosbie made a social visit to the ground at the age of eighty-three. As he perused the surroundings he was probably in blissful ignorance that his transfer had paid for the place.

With no fears as to tenure, serious consideration was then given to Mr Leitch's report. Sympathetic as ever, W.G. Walker & Sons permitted the use of an additional piece of ground to aid the pending development. It was anticipated that adopting the Leitch plan would make it "one of the best equipped football grounds in the provinces."

These were the main points in the report.

The scheme necessitates an alteration in the position of the playing pitch. Instead of sloping across the ground as at present, it will run parallel with Tryfield Place, the street running off Somerset Road on the south side of the ground.

The size of the playing pitch will be 110 yards by 70 yards which is somewhat larger than the existing area.

A border 15-feet wide will be provided between the pitch and the face of the enclosing barriers.

The pitch will run almost due east to west.

On the north side, adjoining the chemical works, extensive banking will be carried out, providing level standing spaces, with crush barriers and gangways.

Similar accommodation, though not carried up to the same elevation, will be provided at the west end adjoining the railway and at the east end abutting on Somerset Road.

The stand buildings will occupy the full length of the south side of the ground next to Tryfield Place.

The dimensions of the stand will be: length 375 feet; breadth 26 feet; height 28 feet.

The accommodation provided at the ground level will comprise, besides the entrances, staircases and pay-boxes to the various divisions of the stand, a room for the directors, a manager's room and office, a referee's room, a trainer's room, a suite of rooms for the home and visiting teams with separate bathrooms and lavatory accommodation, and a gymnasium.

On the upper floor there will be a terraced stand with the following seating accommodation: Unreserved 1,566: reserved 984: directors' private stand 42; total 2,592.

In front of the stand will be a reserved standing space, partly sunk below the level of the playing pitch, giving accommodation for 3,200.

In an intermediate floor underneath the sloping stand will be a six-feet wide distributing passage, giving access to all parts of the stand. It will be utilised also for the purpose of transferring from one division of the stand to another.

The stand will be substantially constructed in brickwork and steel. It will be roofed over with a considerable protection in front by a segmental roof supported on front pillars at wide intervals, giving an uninterrupted view of the whole field.

The holding capacity of the ground will be between 30,000 and 35,000.

The plans were impressive but the estimated cost was unaffordable. Even the stand as a separate entity had a projected cost of £8,000. The directorate had a strong liking for the proposals, notwithstanding that financial constraints would necessitate some modification. It was decided to proceed on the basis of a smaller stand containing 1,345 seats and extending it as and when the future prosperity of the club should permit. The construction of the Family Stand extension in 1989 took it nearer to Mr Leitch's vision. Despite being a leader in his field the eminent gent displayed a degree of optimism in visualising a capacity exceeding 30,000.

Yet even the watered down version of the project was a vast undertaking and it would be four years before the work would get underway, other than that required to remove the cycle track. The fear of affordability was allayed when another spectacular piece of transfer activity took place. On 19th November, 1921, Manchester United created what was then, for them, a club record fee by signing Neil McBain for £4,600. That was enough to pay for the stand, albeit that the eventual cost of the overall development touched £6,000. It was all quite extraordinary. The sale of Johnny Crosbie paid for the ground and the sale of Neil McBain paid for the stand! In November 1923 Willie Gibson was sold to Newcastle United for £2,500. Neither of these transfers were enforced upon the players in order to acquire the by now obvious requirement for funding. Crosbie and Gibson were transfer listed at their own request and an offer was made for McBain that could not be refused. Yet the delay in starting the work was attributable to a nervousness about paying for it. It is difficult to escape the conclusion that, without all that transfer income, the board would have reneged and the plans would have remained on paper.

In February 1920 the demolition of the once famed cycle track got underway. There was an ulterior motive in doing this part of the work with all haste. On 28th February, 1920, Armadale were due at Ayr for a Scottish Cup third round replay. Despite Armadale only having

Central League status a massive crowd was expected. The expectation materialised with an attendance of 10,500. In time for this tie a section of the cycle track was removed at the Somerset Road end. The cleared area created additional capacity which was occupied by more than a thousand standing spectators. If ever there was a time for a good Scottish Cup run this was it. Income was crucial. Non league Armadale won the tie 1-0!

The removal of the cycle track had started even before planning permission was approved. It was a moot point. The track had outlived its use anyway. On Friday, 26th March, 1920, the application was considered at a sitting of the Ayr Dean of Guild Court. The application was on the basis of Archibald Leitch's full plan rather than that subsequently altered to allow for a stand of more modest dimensions. After consideration of the entire minutiae Dean of Guild Stewart concluded: "Plans for the erection of a new stand and other important construction work at Somerset Park, Ayr, the ground of Ayr United Football Club Ltd., are passed, subject to some minor adjustments." There was neither procrastination nor a requirement for multiple consultations back then.

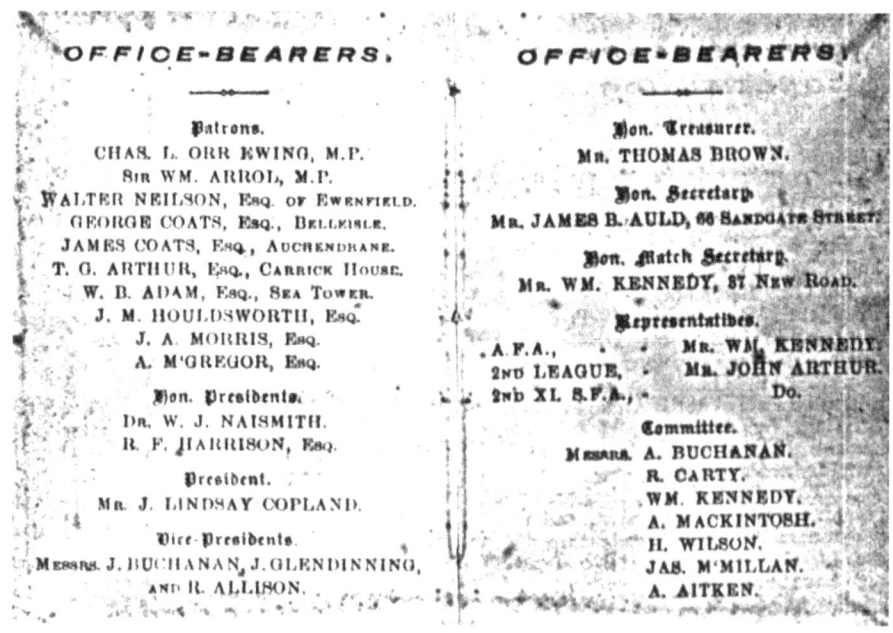

*In 1923 J. Lindsay Copland and James Auld considered the Somerset Park renovations to be "mutilation" because it was the undoing of work they had personally been involved in back in 1897. Here we see their names on the list of Ayr FC office bearers in 1897.*

The whole idea, although popular in the main, met with disfavour from some veterans of the former Ayr FC. Several years later, on 12th January, 1923, J. Lindsay Copland gave a speech at an Ayr FC reunion. In that speech he referred to "the mutilation of Somerset Park." At the time of the 1897 overhaul Mr Copland was the Ayr FC president. Also present at that function was James Auld who, in 1897, had the distinction of being an honorary secretary of the club. Mr Auld did not stand up and speak at the 1923 dinner and it was probably just as well. He was in total accord with the perception of mutilation. In his prime Mr Auld had been the 220-yards champion of Scotland and he had a cast iron reason for being bitter about the destruction of the track. He had put a lot of work into designing it. So proud was he of the finished article that a journalist commented that he looked on the track as his offspring.

At the Annual General Meeting on 31st May, 1920, there was an amusing interlude in response to a question by shareholder Harry Murray. Mr Murray had been the club secretary from Ayr United's inception in May 1910 until May 1914. He had a flair for administration and worked as a clerk in the commissary department of the county buildings. Mr Murray made so bold as to ask the chairman whether the terms on which Somerset Park had been acquired could be divulged. The chairman replied: "We paid £2,500 for it." James MacDonald, the secretary-manager, intervened to say: "At least we agreed to pay that sum. We did not pay it." This prompted laughter to brighten up the somewhat soporific proceedings.

At the outset of season 1920/21 yet more standing capacity was available. It had been created by the cycle track being removed at the railway end during the summer. The holding capacity of the ground was vital. Visits from Rangers, Celtic and Kilmarnock were liable to put it to the test. Scottish Cup visits from virtually anyone also had the potential for a busy ground. 10,500 for a replay against non league Armadale! Between planning consent being granted and the work being completed, the ground record was broken twice. 27th January, 1923, Scottish Cup second round, Ayr United 2 Rangers 0 – 15,853 : 9th February, 1924, Scottish Cup second round, Ayr United 1 Kilmarnock 0 – 16,721.

DUNDEE AND AYR UNITED PLAYERS AND OFFICIALS.

*When Ayr United visited Dundee for a league fixture on 17th September, 1921, the new stand at Dens Park was formally opened. In commemoration of the event a joint team photograph was taken. It was an Archibald Leitch stand. Somerset Park was three years away from the opening of a Leitch structure.*

The grandiose plans were essential rather than cosmetic. In January 1924, at the Ayr FC reunion, chairman Lawrence Gemson was scathing in his criticism of his own club's facilities. He went so far as to express embarrassment at some of the things that counterparts at other clubs had said about "our poor little stand". His opinion was that other clubs' facilities were palatial by comparison. Not holding back, he pressed home his point by saying that, bad though it looked on the outside, it was even worse on the inside. The pavilion, the accommodation for the players and the baths were all inadequate according to Mr Gemson. It embarrassed him too to wonder what the players thought when entering the dressing rooms of opposition clubs. He was emphatic that the stand at Somerset Park had "served its day".

In ridiculing the existing state of Somerset Park, Mr Gemson had an ulterior motive. Having established the urgency for change, he went on to outline a plan to "issue debenture shares at a tempting rate of interest." He continued: "The finances will return to the board and that will mean the difference between opulence and the hand-to-mouth existence that the club is bound to go through for the want of the extra revenue that a big stand will bring us."

It was clear that the project could no longer be reneged upon. In regard to the lingering financial doubt it was hoped that the share issue would liquidate any debt accrued in 1924.

During the 1923/24 season the fear of the big financial commitment manifested itself in a way that implied panic. In the summer of 1923 James MacDonald quit as manager, a role heavy in secretarial duties. Harry Murray was approached. He was the man mentioned on an earlier page because he asked at the 1920 Annual General Meeting whether the cost of buying Somerset Park could be revealed. In secretarial, clerical and administrative matters he had few superiors and he agreed to return on a part time basis but he was not appointed as secretary-manager. Weeks later that job was given to Jimmy Richardson who had vast experience as a player. He is Ayr United's third highest scorer of league goals and he was returning to the fold having been transferred to Millwall two years earlier. In season 1912/13 he had won the Football League with Sunderland. At this time secretarial duties and managerial responsibilities comprised one role. If this was Jimmy Richardson's job then why was Harry Murray brought in at this time? Here is why. With the club close to committing to a vast financial outlay it was considered that there was a danger of reaching a highly precarious position. His one and only role was to steer

*The grand opening on 13th September, 1924.*

the club away from a financial abyss. Quite how this could be done by clerical expertise is a confusing question but this was Harry Murray. This was not the biggest drama in his life. In September 1915 he had to be shipped home due to injuries received while fighting in the Dardanelles. He survived that battle and in 1923/24 he was successful in weaving his magic to avoid the metaphorical battle of Ayr United's finances. How did he do it? In early May 1924 it was reported that: "The debenture issue has been very well received. The response made to the appeal will allow the long deferred ground and stand extension scheme to be put in hand very soon." In the following month he went back to just being a supporter.

*Archibald Leitch would perhaps not have recognised this 2023 image but would no doubt have approved of the modifications.*

At the Annual General Meeting on 2nd May a pledge was made that the work would soon get underway. It did. Rapid progress was made during May only for the momentum to be halted by a builders' strike in June. After the tools were picked up again the work went on apace. By the last week in July the iron framework of the new stand was well advanced. On most days the number of men working at Somerset Park was twenty or more. They worked hectically at the multitude of tasks. These tasks were grass cutting, wheeling earth, excavating and preparing the banking. Rotating the pitch 45° necessitated the laying of fresh turf at the north-west corner and the corner near the main entrances. The playing pitch complied with the plan to make it 110 yards by 70 yards and there was a slight alteration to the plan for a border of fifteen feet. In reality it became thirteen feet consisting of a grass verge of six feet and a cinder track (for training purposes) of seven feet. By reclaiming land on the far side of the ground it was anticipated that the north terrace alone would have capacity for 10,500. The estimated overall capacity had now been revised to 25,000 rather than the previously giddy estimates of between 30,000 and 35,000.

All else complied according to the vision, albeit the vision modified from that of Archibald Leitch. The turf laid to ensure the new shape knitted perfectly. A home match was scheduled for the start of the 1924/25 season. It was a First Division fixture against Third Lanark on 16th August. It was hoped that it would be played at Somerset Park. Alas it was nothing more than hope. On the eve of the season the *Ayrshire Post* reported: "But for the unfortunate, futile and disastrous building strike the work at Somerset Park might have been far enough advanced to permit of the season being opened there even if the stand was not available. It was not to be, however, and Beresford Park will be the scene of the encounter tomorrow."

Season tickets were valid also for reserve matches at Beresford Park but it had not been anticipated that it would be the scene of First Division action. For season 1924/25 these season tickets were priced at seventeen shillings (85p) for the ground and forty shillings (£2) or fifty shillings (£2.50) for the stand, the lesser stand price being for shareholders only. This was in an age when relatively few could afford to pay up front for the season. A crowd estimated at 7,000 turned up for the opener against Third Lanark. At one time the queue to get in stretched all the way across to the Ayrshire and Galloway Hotel while the season ticket holders had a swift entry via a designated gate off Beresford Lane. At the Annual General

Meeting in May the point was raised that the club needed home gates of no less than 6,000. In the interests of financial stability this crowd bode well. A 0-0 draw in what was described as a poor game did not bode so well. On the Wednesday evening the supporters retraced their steps to Beresford Park for league fixture number two but in far lesser numbers. In a 1-0 defeat against Airdrie the crowd was put at 4,000.

More optimistically the team had a 3-2 win away to Hearts on the following Saturday, this good feeling being combined with the knowledge that the construction work was close to being signed off. Yet one more league fixture would require to be played at Beresford Park. Ayr United 3 Aberdeen 3 drew an attendance exceeding the benchmark 6,000. In relation to the building work an away fixture offered some respite (Motherwell 1 Ayr United 1) but for the next again fixture it was vital that Somerset Park was ready. The visit of Rangers was far from conducive to Beresford Park.

Wet weather rendered the park lush and the only incomplete work was internal and mainly in relation to the boardroom, dressing rooms and the room for the match officials. The *Ayrshire Post* waxed lyrical at the prospect of the reopening: "One of the football tit-bits is announced when the redoubtable Rangers supply the opposition to Ayr United. More than ordinary interest centres in the meeting at this time as the visit of the Light Blues is to synchronise with the opening of Greater Somerset, an event in itself which is sure to be an added attraction."

So the stage was set for the big day on 13th September, 1924. Or was it? Monday, 8th September, had to be overcome first of all. That was the date of a Town Council meeting at which the club's application to open the stand required to be formally passed. Since Archibald Leitch had formulated the plans surely nothing could go wrong. To give it a football analogy the process just had to be a penalty kick. As anyone who has watched football will know, penalty kicks can be missed. It all hinged on Mr Young's report. Mr Young was the burgh surveyor and he was very meticulous when it came to detail. His report contained the following criticisms.

The description of the building lodged does not comply with the plans as regards the seating accommodation. A plan should be lodged showing the extent of the seating in the central section where 600 tip-up chairs are now to be installed instead of plain seat boards as shown on the plans and also the other seating in the two wings which provides for 745 seats.

It is essential that the plans are properly adjusted immediately so that it might be referred to in the future should any question of overcrowding of the different sections occur.

The position, height and construction of the barricades between the different sections of the seating should also be shown as well as their relation to the staircases.

There should be two staircases to each section of the stand . As proposed the two wing sections would only have one staircase each.

Either the woodwork is treated to make it non inflammable or fire appliances are installed to the approval of the firemaster.

No WCs are shown on the plan for the public in the stand and in the enclosure. These should be provided.

Until the above matters have been adjusted I recommend that approval under section 166 of the Burgh Police (Scotland) Act, 1892, should be delayed.

There could be no doubting that the burgh surveyor was good at his job. It was tough on Ayr United that the club was up against a man who was conversant with the Burgh Police (Scotland) Act of 1892.

The report was compared to a bomb exploding. It was Monday and the big game was on Saturday. Was there any hope? At the end of the report there was some hope, albeit a glimmer. The conclusion was:

"In view of the unfinished state of the structure and the application to use same on 13th September, I would respectfully suggest that an early meeting of the Dean of Guild Court and the directors of the club should take place at the site so that some definite arrangements can be made before any approval of the Town Council and Dean of Guild Court is given."

Time was of the essence and the suggested meeting took place the next day at Somerset Park. Mercifully an amicable and satisfactory settlement was reached. It was confirmed, with four days to spare, that the field and stand would be available.

On the day of the match there was a formal opening ceremony for the stand. It commenced shortly after 2pm at which time the crowd was well short of the eventual estimated figure of 17,000. The observation that the weather clerk was on his best behaviour was a euphemism for it being sunny. Many guests were invited to the formal proceedings, most of whom were football officials or civic heads of the burgh. Douglas Bowie, the Ayr United chairman, presided. During his speech he said: "It will be the endeavour of the board to build up a team sufficiently strong to give our friends and opponents Rangers a keen run for the championship flag." This induced laughter as was his intention.

Tom White of Celtic then stepped forward. He was there in his capacity of president of the Scottish Football Association. He said that he had great pleasure in assisting in the opening of "this magnificent stand" then went on to mention that: "Right down the east coast Aberdeen, Dundee, Raith Rovers, Hibs and Hearts have all spent money on improving their ground and stand accommodation but it redounds to the credit of Ayr United that in building the stand they have not had behind them the industrial population of these centres mentioned and consequently their task has been greater by comparison. It is a wonderful thing for me to see this stand as it was only about eighteen months ago that I heard there was a question of the club living or dying. I hope Ayr United win today, not because I want to see Rangers beaten (laughter) and I trust they will go on winning until they meet Celtic (laughter)."

When J. Lindsay Copland came forward to speak there must have been some trepidation or even downright fear. Please remember that he was the chap who, in the previous year, had publically referred to the project as "the mutilation of Somerset Park." Somewhat strangely he had been asked to propose "The town and trade of Ayr." He stuck to his remit rigidly and a little sycophantly: "It is gratifying that the new stand should be inaugurated in the presence of the civic heads of the burgh." Either he had relented or thought it politic not to speak his mind.

To Mrs Bowie, the chairman's wife, went the honour of cutting the tape to formally open the stand. When the match got underway the light mood got banished in a 4-0 defeat. Five months earlier the first ever international had taken place at Wembley and, in a 1-1 draw, the Scotland full-backs were the Ayr United full-backs Jock Smith and Phil McCloy. Overall the Ayr team of 1924/25 was rich in individual talent and, together with the boost in morale from the new surrounds, there was an optimism which seemed realistic. Alas the confidence proved to be a hoax. An adventurous plan had been implemented but the season ended in relegation. In adversity there is a tendency to adopt the default view that it could have been worse. It was chilling that Tom White, in his speech, mentioned that he had heard of Ayr United's threat to survival. The threat would have been even more perilous had not Harry Murray been recruited temporarily to mastermind a share issue. The club's status could indeed have been radically worse than that conferred by having to compete in the Second Division.

*Chapter Four*

# The Railway End

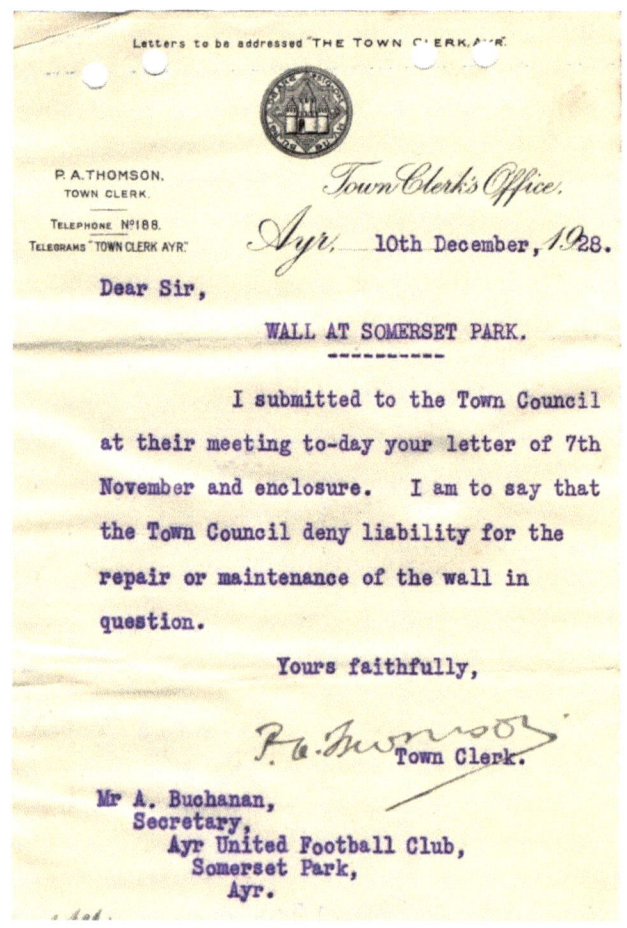

*On 10th December, 1928, the Town Clerk absolved the council of responsibility for the repair of a wall at Somerset Park.*

There is a certain irony that the public were so embittered by the standard of football that they formed a supporters' club which would ultimately benefit Ayr United in terms of helping to finance improved facilities at Somerset Park. The help would last for decades and by the 1950s it would hit overdrive. On Monday, 14th February, 1927, a representative meeting of fans was held in the local Palais de Danse. Season 1925/26 resulted in a third place finish in the Second Division and in 1926/27 form dipped to such an extent that eighth place was the club's lot. On that February night the discussions about the team were less than cordial. Action was required and action happened. The idea of starting a supporters' club met with consensus. It was agreed that this initiative would in no way be antagonistic towards the directors. The aim was to encourage and support them. A meeting was soon convened by the newly formed Ayr United Supporters' Club. It took place in the Town Hall on the Thursday evening of 3rd March. Provost Gould presided over a packed hall. Despite the prevailing positivity the players got barracked at the next home match which bore the spectacle of a 2-0 defeat against Stenhousemuir. Yet the organised body of supporters remained true to their mission statement and worked actively to provide practical help.

By 1929 it was known that the board had a desire to build a covered enclosure at the railway end of the ground. On 15th July that year the Ayr United Supporters' Club staged a sports meeting at Somerset Park. It was a thoroughly well organised event and the proceeds were earmarked towards the cost of a proposed enclosure. Proposed enclosure? It may be stretching the point to suggest that it had even reached the status of a proposal in 1929. The idea was little more than precisely that – an idea. Success depended on the ability to raise the required funds. The sports event assisted greatly towards that aim. It took place in the evening of Glasgow Fair Monday which happened to be the hottest day of the year so far and the town was packed with excursionists. The main event that night was a Boxers versus Jockeys football match. It was a novel spectacle which the boxers won 6-5. One of the jockeys who scored was the legendary Harry Wragg whose name is now synonymous with rhyming slang for Partick Thistle (Harry Wraggs – Jags). It was refereed by Dixie Dean, the Everton marksman whose name remains written in legend. In fact a sprint for footballers that night was won by the great man. There is no surviving documentary proof of how much money the event raised yet by implication it can be assumed to have been significant. By equal implication it can be assumed that it was nonetheless a long way from the amount required to get the contractors on site. This argument is borne out by the four-year gap until it materialised. The formation of the Supporters' Club proved to be a catalyst for an Ayr United Ladies Supporters' Club. This was a beneficial development because the ladies set about tackling the same objective as their male counterparts. Fund raising for the enclosure was now being attacked on two fronts.

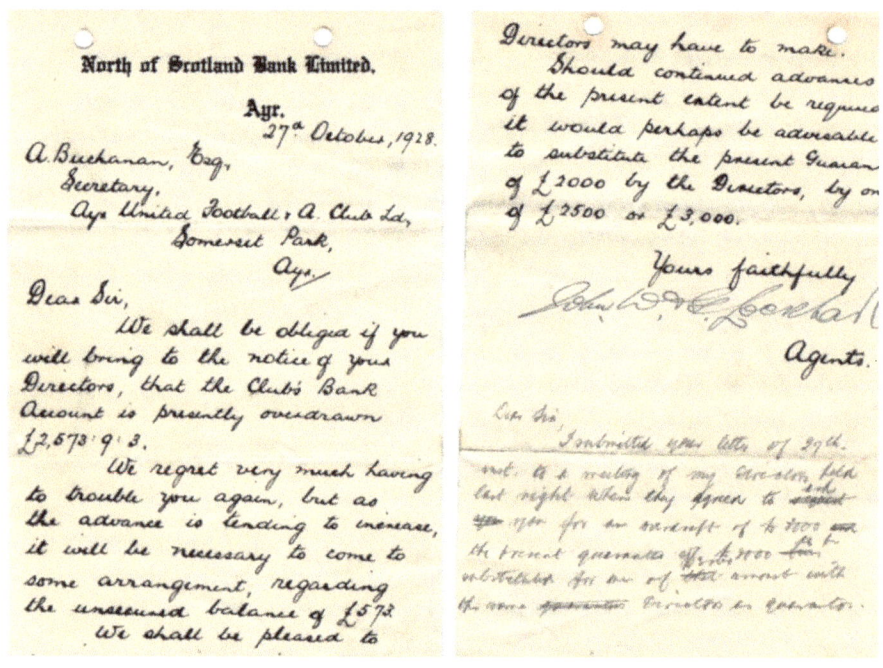

*The grand scale of renovation created an impact on the club's finances for years afterwards. This letter from 27th October, 1928, diplomatically requests the club to address the issue of being overdrawn by £2,573 : 9s : 3d.*

In May 1932 Ayr United turned down a proposal for dog racing at the ground. It would have been financially rewarding but far from aesthetically pleasing. Besides, dog tracks were unpopular with all but the main enthusiasts for that sport. On 25th August, 1933, the Ayr Dean of Guild Court met to consider a petition by the Ayr Greyhound Stadium Company for setting up a greyhound racing track at Limekiln Road. It was passed. The decision of the Dean of Guild Court was not in accord with the court of public opinion. In the local newspaper columns it was opined that: "It is likely to bring unsavoury characters about the place.

Had it been proposed for the south side of the river it would have got its quietus at once. Why should it be foisted on the people over there?" In the fullness of time a greyhound did race at Somerset Park. Only one! When Morton were here for a league fixture on the night of 1st March, 1994, Brian Bilsland struck the winner in the closing minutes and amidst the celebrations a greyhound raced onto the field. It is not a dog you would have wished to back in a race. Suffice to say that Malky Shotton caught it whereupon he carried it off the field.

*The Railway End enclosure. Opened in 1933 but with a few embellishments in this 2023 image.*

By the start of the 1932/33 season the Ladies Supporters' Club had a flourishing membership of 250. The season opened with a First Division fixture at home to Queen's Park and, before kick-off, Mrs Huntly, their president, unfurled a flag which the women had donated. In January 1933 it was reported that: "The Ayr United Ladies Supporters' Club have donated a further sum to the football club and this has been laid aside as the nucleus of a fund for the erection of a covered terracing for the one shilling spectator." Notwithstanding the old saying that you cannot do bad by doing good, a negative spin was put on this development. With the respective organisations working independently of each other one journalist was of a mind that there was friction. This was the latest in a series of donations from the women and it drew the following criticism from the *Ayrshire Post*. It was headed 'A Snub'.

> "The decision of the Ayr United directors to lay aside the latest donation from the Ladies Supporters' Club as the nucleus of a fund for the erection of a covered terracing looks like a snub for the male Supporters' Club. It is a pity that all concerned could not let bygones be bygones and get together to work for the erection of a covering. By co-operation the football club and the two supporters' clubs could soon get the money required. As we have suggested before, by running special attractions, such as a visit from a prominent English club, money could be speedily gathered. As things are the covered terracing is as far off as ever."

It can only be guessed as to whether the friction was real or perceived. Yet any spirit of competition between those two quite distinct organisations could have been viewed as advantageous in the matter of fundraising.

In early August 1933 a momentous announcement was made: "Ayr United are definitely going forward with the erection of a covered terracing for the ordinary shilling spectator. Such an erection will ensure the spectator against a wetting when the weather is uncongenial and at the same time ensure the club of the support of the spectator." It would have the capacity to cover 3,000 spectators. Charles Nair, an architect, prepared and gifted the plans. The board considered this to be phase one of a larger scheme that would see the new enclosure getting extended so that there would be covered accommodation for 7,000 fans (including the 1,345 in the stand) and the ultimate goal was to provide covered accommodation for the entire ground. It was considered that Ayr United were pioneers because other clubs who had recently constructed covered enclosures had done so for the gratification of those who attended greyhound racing rather than for the football supporters. The point was emphasised by the comment that: "Ayr United have very wisely left such a controversial 'sport' as greyhound racing severely alone." Not just alone but severely alone! Note too the cheeky punctuation on the word 'sport'. In retrospect this was a tenuous reason for claiming some sort of moral high ground besides being historically inaccurate on the question of the prime motive of those other clubs. It was reminiscent of 1924 when the claim was made that the new stand was more worthy of praise than relatively recent structures elsewhere because Ayr and district had a lesser population. In the final analysis the donations from the respective supporters' groups were £230 (men) and £130 (ladies). It was a splendid effort all round, even in face of accusations that it would have been more beneficial to have implemented a combined effort.

*In the gap between the track wall and the pillar in the foreground, a turnstile was sited between 1933 and 1963. It was for the purpose of an additional charge to gain entry to the covered accommodation. When repanelling this end of the enclosure the liberty was taken to remove the panel that was in place from the top of the wall to ground level. With the old turnstile long since removed the bottleneck became a memory.*

The official opening of the new structure coincided with a league visit from Kilmarnock. 2.45pm was considered sufficient time to deal with the pomp, ceremony and speechifying. It began with chairman Alex Moffat introducing James Fleming, president of the Scottish Football Association. In his speech Mr Fleming was fulsome in his praise, albeit with a hint of condescension.

"I wish to congratulate the Ayr club on their catering for the ordinary spectator. For too long he who is commonly known as the 'bob' man has been sadly neglected, and this scheme will add to the comfort of the man who is the most loyal supporter of any club. I understand that this scheme is but a small beginning to a scheme the directors have in view. Football clubs, like other concerns, cannot exist on fair weather supporters. The Ayr club by this venture are hoping for increased support, and when the scheme is completed it is hoped that everyone who attends games will look on in comfort, even in wet weather. I understand that the scheme has had a measure of support from the supporters' clubs of both sexes. I urge these clubs to carry on with the good work. I have much pleasure in declaring the enclosure open, and I wish the Ayr club the success its efforts richly merit."

In his reply Alex Moffat said:

"It has long been the dream of the Ayr United directors to fully enclose the park but something has always come in the way. We have aimed high, however, and we have achieved something. For this we are indebted to a number of very good friends and I take the opportunity of thanking the Ayr United Supporters' Clubs. I might say that the ladies contributed £130 towards the enclosure and the men £230. I hope that the clubs will not stop at that, but that there will be keen, healthy rivalry and that the ladies will endeavour to catch up on the men, and the men maintain their lead (laughter). I hope that the supporters of the club will appreciate the efforts the directors have made on their behalf. I also hope that the directors can look forward confidently to getting full support, even when the weather is not too good. I thank Mr Nair, the architect, for the services he has given free, and I hope that before very long we will have another job for him at the same rate of remuneration (laughter). I thank the contractors and three directors – Douglas Bowie (vice president of the Scottish Football Association), Mr Drinnan and Baillie Govan."

In reference to the mention of Baillie Govan, this was David Govan and he was several years away from having his status elevated. On 31st March, 1936, he was elected as Provost of Prestwick. In his capacity as an

Ayr United director he would have been most useful when the enclosure project was being undertaken. He was a builder to trade and it is just possible that some of you reading this may even live in a Govan-built bungalow.

On the opening day, the occasion of a 1-1 draw with Kilmarnock, admission to the new enclosure was free but from that date on there was a charge of tuppence. The logic to this was clarified by the board:

"There will be a very nominal figure for admission to the shelter and when by this means a sufficient sum is collected, an addition will be made so that it will accommodate a greater number."

By the 1963/64 season the initial charge of tuppence had become a shilling (sixpence for juveniles). In late November 1963 the charge was scrapped altogether but the club did not implement the promise to extend. The perilous state of the finances meant that the pledge could not be contemplated. Were the directors of 1963 aware of the pledge made in 1933? Alex Moffat would have been. He was on the Ayr United board from 1923 until 1965. Here was a man who could have testified to the evolution of Somerset Park better than anybody. His Ayr FC debut was as far back as 19th March, 1898, when he played at left-back in a 4-0 win at home to Paisley Academicals in a friendly.

Your writer can recall the time when it was required to pay extra to enter the covered enclosure at the railway end. Back then it was the only area of covered terracing. It used to give rise to farcical scenes. If rain came on during a match terracing dwellers such as myself would have the option of either getting soaked or scrambling towards the turnstile located at the bottleneck bordering the enclosure and the north terrace. On occasion the rain would cease while people were still queuing and, en masse, the queue would get abandoned. Your writer never once joined the scramble to get in. Sixpence was too valuable to a juvenile.

## Chapter Five

# Shoulders to the Wheel

From an earlier chapter you may recall the expression 'shoulders to the wheel'. It was used by Walter Lindsay when reminiscing about Ayr FC moving from Springvale Park to Beresford Park in 1884 and from there to Somerset Park in 1888. Dismantling, transporting and rebuilding timber structures had been physically taxing therefore he could have been using the phrase literally or metaphorically. The 'shoulders to the wheel' analogy appeared in the columns of the local press again. That was in 1945 in the context of Old Lady Somerset requiring a major tidy-up. Not that you would have seen a mention of Old Lady Somerset in 1945. This fictitious title originated in your writer's imagination yet it seems so apt.

On the Thursday evening of 30th May, 1940, Ayr United's Annual General Meeting saw the business concluded in five minutes. Britain was gripped by the fear of a German invasion. Three days earlier they had taken Calais. The chairman, Andrew Wright, said: "Football next year is in the lap of the Gods." On Saturday, 1st June, Ayr United beat Aberdeen 2-1 at home to win the Scottish Second X1 Cup on a 3-2 aggregate. It was significant because first teams took part in that season's competition. On the other hand it was insignificant because the evacuation of Dunkirk was taking place while the match was in progress. The attendance was less than 3,000. People had a lot more to worry about. Mindful of this it was announced that: "The club is closing down in the meantime." It was a vague timescale which implied that the closure would last for the duration.

Ayr United's next match was a 'B' Division fixture at home to Airdrie on 11th August, 1945. Since playing on 1st June, 1940, the gap without a game extended to five years and seventy-one days. During those years football still took place at Somerset Park. War time representative matches were played and by 1944/45 the ground was being used by two local junior clubs for home matches. These clubs were Ayr Newton Rovers and Scottish Stampworks and Engineeering.

When the course of the war indicated an almost certain victory there were local stirrings of interest in Ayr United making a comeback.

In February 1945 ex-Baillie Willison raised the issue at a meeting of the Town Council: "I hope that the directors will do their utmost to put Ayr United and Ayr itself once more on the map." In the following month there was a hint of a planned return when volunteers from the 9th Holding Battalion, based at Ayr Racecourse, moved in to tackle the weeds on the terracing. This was far from a one-off solution and they returned intermittently up until October. There was an unanticipated consequence when the football did get underway. Discarded cigarette ends reacted with the weed killer to create small flames which had to be stamped out. In March 1945 goalkeeper Alex Corbett was signed from Annbank United. This was a certain sign that football would be returning to Somerset Park. Albeit that there were players still on the retained list from 1940 this new signing was a clear statement of intent. Yet it was not until a meeting on 29th May that it was confirmed that the club would be engaging in football in 1945/46. An advertisement for a new manager was responded to successfully by Bob Ferrier who was appointed on 20th June. Rapid team building was one remit but the secretarial part of his job was both daunting and urgent.

The major priority was getting Somerset Park derequisitioned. During the war the dressing rooms had been taken over by the council for cleansing purposes for ARP wardens (air raid precautions). The requisition had been made by use of emergency measures. Although this occurred compulsorily the council paid rent which was just as well. At the Annual General Meeting on 14th June it was seen that Ayr United sat £5,567 in debt. In July the council asked the club to formulate any claims for damage caused by the granting of the facilities. The club replied that they would make no claim provided that Ayr United could keep the showers and sprays which the council had built. As a sweetener the board also offered to forego payment of the previous month's rent. It was all agreed.

In the summer of 1946 William Graham was asked to returf the goal areas. He courteously obliged. His experience in this field came from being the greenkeeper at Prestwick St.Nicholas Golf Club. One year later he was appointed as the Somerset Park groundsman from a dozen applicants. He immersed himself in the job straight away. Repeating what he had done the year before, he returfed the goal areas. Other parts were resown. The track was levelled, this work being done by two German prisoners of war. This work on the track was a big task. Between the two of them they removed one hundred tons of ashes. Red blaes then got laid and the track was rolled. The complete exercise considerably enhanced the appearance of the track. This reference to POWs may seem surprising since this was the summer of 1947. Their camp was at Doonfoot and there were some excellent footballers amongst their number. In a summer friendly that year they put a team together to play junior club Ayr Newton Rovers. Under the name of Germany X1 they won 10-2.

The neglect suffered during the war years was further addressed during the 1947 close season. Trainer Davie Logan and his assistant Willie Hunter added fresh coats of paint, varnish and distemper to the dressing rooms and other rooms beneath the stand. To complete the summer of change the board installed a new loudspeaker system comprising five speakers spread throughout the enclosure. The main function was to give information to spectators. Yet the supposedly secondary function was even better. That function was a programme of music before the kick-off and at half-time. The system was first used on the evening of 13th August, 1947. It was a 'B' Division fixture which resulted Ayr United 0 Albion Rovers 2. Was the music enough to soothe angry passions?

The Supporters' Association had been revived in 1946. By the start of the 1947/48 season it had a membership topping 700. All manner of trades were represented within that membership and there was a willingness to offer their services for the overall development of Somerset Park. The impending new decade would see this proved to spectacular effect. This reformed organisation incorporated both genders rather than the two distinct supporters' clubs which existed before the war.

In September 1948 the board came up with a plan to remove the bottleneck at the north-west entrance to the railway end. A triangular piece of adjoining ground had been acquired and it was considered that this would cut off the troublesome corner and, at the same time, increase capacity. This plan was made known at the same time as another plan to extend the enclosure at the railway end in order to meet the stand. This would have complied with the 1933 vision to gradually increase the covered accommodation and would have had the additional advantage of cutting out the nuisance of wind swirl in that corner. These plans were made known to the public but neither was implemented.

*A deserved break for the cheerful volunteers who built the track wall in the summer of 1950. In front of the group you will see the rotted fencing that they had already removed.*

*Chapter Six*

# Ayr United Supporters' Association

## THE MASSIVE 1950s INPUT

In May 1950 the Supporters' Association put out the following appeal.

### HELP NEEDED

"Volunteer bricklayers and plasterers are wanted to help in building a wall round the track at Somerset Park. The work, which is now underway, is being undertaken as a result of the original fence having rotted and gradually fallen away. Anyone wishing to assist should apply to Mr Muir, at the park, any evening after seven."

The Mr Muir referred to was John Muir. His grandson, David Kennedy, became an Ayr United player. David made his first team debut on 28th February, 1987. There was a quick and positive response to the appeal. Within a week news emanated that good progress had been made already. There was a confidence that the wall would be completed before the start of season 1950/51. Albeit that the labour was voluntary the materials had to be paid for. To this end the Supporters' Association came up with a scheme allowing the fans to sponsor a brick for a shilling. The initiative was slickly marketed as a bob-a-brick campaign. As an alternative people were quite at liberty to make a straight donation.

From the columns of the *Ayrshire Post* came confirmation that the work had been completed ahead of time.

"When the Ayr United players resume training on 25th July, they'll hardly recognise the Somerset Park of last season. The new Supporters' Club wall is complete and its creamy-white paint sets off the red running track and the green of the playing field which has been returfed in the centre and goal areas."

It was such a solid structure that it sat round the perimeter of the track for sixty-nine years. Although it was ultimately demolished and replaced the rationale had nothing to do with decay. In April 2019 the wall constructed in 1950 got replaced at the behest of South Ayrshire Council. You will be spared the fine detail laid out in a series of technical reports which expounded on a wealth of regulations. The replacement wall of 2019 was a fine asset yet in mentioning this it seems appropriate to praise the quality and solidity of its predecessor. It was built on toil, sweat, craftsmanship, dedication and lashings of tea with piles of home baking. The sustenance was provided by the lady committee members.

Despite the volunteer labour and financial support from the public, the wall project still left a financial deficit. On the evening of 16th August, 1950, the visit of Kilmarnock attracted a crowd estimated at 15,000 for a League Cup sectional tie. With a view to clearing the deficit a collection was made at this match.

*When the volunteers of 1950 built the track wall a gap was left for vehicular access, typically a tractor for pitch maintenance. Some of you may also recall the little invalid cars accessing their stance on the track via this route.*

The Supporters' Association then conceived an idea to help finance team matters. This was at a time when building initiatives were still very much at the forefront of their priorities. Club director George Sutherland took up the baton and implemented the idea. In pursuit of providing the financial backing necessary to get the club into 'A' Division, a free gift auction sale was held on the Saturday evening of 23rd December, 1950. The venue was the horse sale ring at Ayr Cattle Market and the crowd looked to be about 2,000. So great was the crush that a loudspeaker was used to make the proceedings audible to people who were accommodated in an adjoining byre. Your writer attended a similar event at that venue in 1970 in aid of the Ayr United floodlight fund but that is a story for a future chapter. In 1950 the prize item was a pedigreed Jersey heifer donated by John Sword. It was purchased by Tom Murray who had been the Ayr Provost between 1943 and 1949. He paid 100 guineas. Calves, poultry, sheep, carpets and furniture were among the items sold. The total accrued was £1,150. Although coming up with the idea but not implementing it, the Supporters' Association co-operated to great effect. This was acknowledged at a dinner at the Prestwick Airport Hotel on 12th February, 1951. It was chaired by Ayr United chairman James Frew and the purpose was by way of a thank you to the people most closely associated with the auction sale. In thanking the main donors and organisers Mr Frew had this to say about the Supporters' Club. "They gave us tremendous help, a finer body of men I don't think I have ever come across." At the risk of diverting from the main topic, please excuse this brief diversion to explain that Mr Frew's grandfather, John Frew, was responsible for the formation of Parkhouse back in 1886. At that time John Frew lived in Park House in Ballantine Drive. It concerned him that boys were playing football on the road so he offered them the use of an adjoining field. The offer was accepted and the team was named after Mr Frew's residence.

Let us now revert to topic. Since the auction sale was aimed at providing finance to strengthen the playing squad, would the Supporters' Club now channel their energies in that direction rather than the development of Somerset Park? Certainly not. Their next building project had already begun several weeks before the thank you dinner. This venture comprised alterations to the terracing and it was underway by January 1951. By now there was a Building Committee which was distinct from the main committee. Volunteers were asked to report on Sundays at 10am. In recent years there had been instances when many supporters had struggled to get a decent view, even on tiptoe. One such example occurred on 5th February,

1949, when Morton visited for a Scottish Cup tie. The fact that it was only a second round tie did not deter an attendance of 20,584 paying spectators with the number of season ticket holders inflating the overall crowd to 21,462. It was almost as if the volunteers of 1951 had the gift of prophecy because Motherwell visited for a Scottish Cup quarter-final on 10th March that year and the crowd was 22,152. In anticipation of the Motherwell tie it was necessary to erect hurriedly built crush barriers. Throughout February the Sunday morning volunteers worked conscientiously and by the month end the objective was well on course. That objective was the construction of stepping with concrete blocks on the north terrace. Once more an appeal went out to the public for financial support to reimburse the cost of materials. On 17th February a collection at the home match with Stirling Albion raised £27. By April the tireless cry for volunteers was still being issued and by 1951/52 the ground was more capable of holding large crowds with less fear of restricted viewing.

Let us now take stock. The Supporters' Association could look back with pride and be satisfied with the work they had done in constructing the wall round the track and improving the terracing. However these people were not of a mind to bask in self congratulatory praise. They were possessed of a single minded determination to enhance the facilities at Somerset Park even more. The thought process was what could be done next. It was considered that Old Lady Somerset would benefit from the construction of a gymnasium.

In June 1951 Ayr Town Council ratified a plan to build a gymnasium in the south-west corner of Somerset Park at an estimated cost of £1,200. Permission was granted for this as well as a plan to erect a new brick boundary wall to enclose additional ground recently acquired on the far side, the projected cost being £450. The wall was far from an insignificant project for the Supporters' Association but the construction of a gymnasium by use of voluntary labour seemed hugely complex, albeit that third party contractors would be used for work requiring a specialist. The potential strain on finances would have been reason enough for reconsidering. Yet the chances of reconsidering were nil. This was a group that would press on undaunted.

In the same month that planning permission was granted, the appeal went out and it was getting to be a familiar one.

# TRADESMEN WANTED

"An appeal for bricklayers, plasterers and labourers is made by the Ayr United Supporters' Association in an effort to complete the building of the new boundary wall before the Festival of Britain cup tie against Cowdenbeath on 25th July. Volunteers will be welcome every Tuesday and Thursday evening from 6.30 – 9.00 and on Sundays from 10.00 – 4.00."

It was already the end of June. Was 25th July an optimistic deadline? Just a little. The wall, at what was popularly known as Walker's Corner, got finished during the Sunday stint on 12th August. What a job it was! It required digging out a foundation six feet deep to carry the wall which reached a height of eighteen feet at one stage and was three feet thick from the foundations to half its height above the ground. It was envisaged that the complete wall between Somerset Park and Walker's would run to approximately 200 yards but the 1951 project was aimed at completing approximately a third of it then holding it in abeyance. Other projects loomed and the wall was held over until 1954. It is not that the scheme was abandoned. This was part of a plan. The Supporters' Association had the proud record of never having abandoned any scheme they had begun.

Now for the big one – the gymnasium to be constructed between the stand and the railway end of the ground. The target for completion was "early in the New Year." They worked like Trojans and it was finished in time to be the venue for the Supporters' Association Christmas draw on the evening of 21st December. At this time the interior was basic. Little or no money was left to fund the cost of all of the planned refinements. The formal handover to Ayr United had yet to take place but the gift made provision for the Supporters' Association to use the premises for social events when not required by the club. This explained the appeal for the donation of a piano or the offer to buy one cheaply.

By March 1952 a rumour circulated that there were strained relations, or even actual disruption, between the directors and the association. John Muir came straight to the point. "We don't know who started this story but it is ridiculous nonsense. Forthcoming events will prove it to be the fallacy it is. We make bold to say that there isn't another organisation in football in the country which holds such a unique position as regards relations between club and supporters and we intend to keep it that way."

In referring to forthcoming events this was a clear reference to the function that had had been arranged for the formal handover of the gymnasium keys. It was held on the Thursday evening of 13th March. Present were the club directors, Supporters' Association officials, team captain Norrie McNeil and members and friends of the Supporters' Association. Mrs Martin, the social convenor, called upon John Muir to hand over the keys. In doing so Mr Muir paid tribute to the people who, by their industry in their leisure hours, had made the building of the gymnasium possible. On receiving the keys, Ayr United chairman James Frew said:

> "This is a proud day for Ayr United Football Club. It really is a terrific effort built out of goodness of heart. There is no supporters' club in Scotland which has done more for their club in the last few years than ours. They built the retaining wall round the playing pitch which put us on the way to having one of the best football stadiums in Scotland and now they have come along with this magnificent gymnasium. There has never been at any time in the history of our club, a finer relationship between the supporters and the board."

*John Muir being conferred with honorary life membership on 27th April, 1954.*

James Frew then wound up by conferring an honorary life membership of Ayr United on John Muir. In asking Mr Muir to accept the honour he said: "It is people like you, who make people like us like people like you." Mr Muir was also presented with a medal to mark the granting of his life membership, albeit that he did not receive it on the night. It was presented a couple of years later (on 27th April, 1954). Compounding the honour was the fact that he was the first life member in the club's history.

Richard Jamieson, the Provost of Newmilns, then stepped up to congratulate the Supporters' Association on a job well done and he congratulated Ayr United on having one of the nicest stadiums in Scotland. Provost Jamieson had been responsible for the gift of tapestry curtains adorning the gymnasium. This may beg the question as to why a Newmilns Provost was involved. The answer is that he was a keen supporter of Ayr United. A social evening followed the formal part of the event. This was all very cordial but several years later the Supporters' Association had to write to the Ayr United board to remind them of one of the main conditions attached to the gift. In January 1956 lights were broken and the club had to be formally reminded that the use of a ball in the gymnasium was not permitted.

*The formal opening of the gymnasium on 13th March, 1952.*

The work of these supporters could not be underestimated, a fact not lost on the Ayr United board. By way of reward for the gymnasium, the directors intimated a decision to take all of the working party of the association to the forthcoming Scotland versus England game and to entertain them at dinner at the Prestwick Airport Hotel on the way back. In the cold light of day the Supporters' Association still had the problem of a red bank balance. On the principle that money makes money, they built catering kiosks within the ground and this was most successful in reducing the deficit. Lady members staffed these kiosks on a voluntary basis on match days.

The complimentary remarks about the stadium were not merely patronising. Old Lady Somerset was indeed looking well. The ground was even chosen to host the World Pipe Band Championship on 28th June, 1952. Despite a last minute deluge of rain there was a crowd estimated at 10,000.

It may have appeared that the work done by the supporters had peaked. This was far from the case. The next idea was, once more, a bold one. Experience had already proven that their bold ideas could always be counted upon to reach fruition. The plan was to relay Ayr United commentaries to local hospitals. In mid-April 1953 this announcement was made.

"As a result of efforts made by the Ayr United Supporters' Association permission to broadcast commentaries on football matches at Somerset Park to patients in Ayr County Hospital and Heathfield Hospital has been granted by the board of management for Southern Ayrshire Hospitals."

*The architect's plan for the broadcasting studio*

```
                    AYR  UNITED  F.C.  SUPPORTERS'  ASSOCIATION

        Income and Expenditure Account for the year ended 31st March, 1959.

              Income                                    Expenditure

Catering                   £ 1716. 3.10   Catering                  £ 1335.19. 8
Socials                         42. 9. 7  Maintenance                    97. 1. 7
Bus Parties                     19.14.10  Building                      424. -. 4
Membership Fees                 31.18. 9  Miscellaneous                  56. 4.10

Programmes -                              Programmes - Printing          286. 5. 5
Sales         £ 257. 9.11
Advertising                               Donations -
  Revenue        284.18. -     542. 7.11  Hospital Relay
Raffle                           6. 5. -    Fund          £ 20. -. -
Savings Account Interest        14. 9. 1  Ambulance Ass.    1. 5. -      21. 5. -
                               _____  Profit                        152.12. 2
                                                                        _____
                              £ 2373. 9. -                             £ 2373. 9. -

                 Assets of Association at 31st March, 1959.

        Saleable Stock                                 £ 61. -. -
        Equipment at written down value
        Works                           £ 30. -. -
        Catering                         100. -. -
        Social                            20. -. -      150. -. -
        Loan to Development Club                         75. -. -
        Savings Account National Bank                   433. -. 3
        Current Account National Bank                   388. 9. 9
        Cash held by Treasurer                           93. 3. 6
                                                       _____
                                                     £ 1200.13. 6

        Less Liabilities

        Sundry Creditors                 £ 56.14. 8
        Funds belonging to
          Wembley Club                     284. 7. 9    341. 2. 5

             Net Assets of Association               £ 859.11. 1


        21st April, 1959.    We certify that we have examined the books of
        Ayr United F.C. Supporters' Association and find them to be correct
        and properly vouched.  We have examined the Bank Statement and Savings
        Account Book and found the balances to be correct.

                        (Sgd.) A. J. FABER   )
                                             )  Auditors.
                        ( "  ) JAMES CAMERON )
```

*The profit on catering for the year ending 31st March, 1959, was close to £400 while the building expenditure was marginally more than £400. As a means of offsetting building costs the catering initiative was successful.*

Much of the work done to get it to this stage had been done by committee man Harry Cattenach. Did he have experience of wireless systems? No, he was a bus driver. He was also a Fifer from Elie but had been driving buses in Ayrshire since 1923. His Fife roots and lack of expertise in this field did not prove a hindrance. He was passionately dedicated to the Ayr United cause and lived just walking distance from the ground at 13 Russell Street. His devotion lasted almost to his dying day. He passed away at the age of 57 on 10th September, 1960, having been recently involved in assisting to set up the Ayr United Development Club which was destined to raise significant funds. To assist the hospital broadcast venture the Ayr United board made available any facility required and there was a promise of full co-operation. Yet again the Supporters' Association faced the threat of frightening expenditure. Yet again Harry Cattenach appealed to the generosity of the public. It was hoped that the installation would be ready in time for the first home match of the 1953/54 season. With the benefit of hindsight you may be told that this deadline had no chance of being achieved. Sentimentally it was thought that the nature of the cause would lead to a deluge of contributions. The projection was that £400 would be required for the installation of the required apparatus and its subsequent upkeep. At the start of July the money raised totalled £103 : 5s : 1½d. Note the ha'penny! The Supporters' Association was already pushing for solvency while still being mindful of the requirement for raising enough money to complete the wall separating the north terrace from Walker's. How could the shortfall be bridged? It helped that the hospital authorities agreed to the use of existing wiring and equipment. Private donations continued to trickle in but the main source of subscriptions came from many of the major local employers who were not averse to collecting tins on their premises. By that means it was viable to set up the installation to cover the male wards in Ayr County Hospital, Heathfield Hospital and the Welfare Home. Merely two committee members were delegated with the responsibility of pulling it off. Not that their colleagues were idle. During the 1953 close season committee men got busy painting Somerset Park inside and out but they did not conform to the club colours and the fans were left with an illusion that they were entering Tynecastle.

By stint of some professional begging enough money was accrued to top the £400 required to proceed with the hospital relay installation. In September 1953 an appeal of a different sort went out.

> "Ayr United Supporters' Association appeal for people with
> clear speaking voices and a good knowledge of football
> to volunteer as commentators for the relay broadcasts to
> Ayr County Council, Heathfield Hospital and the Welfare
> Home."

The hopefuls were auditioned in the hope that someone would be able to emulate the likes of Raymond Glendinning or Peter Thomson, both of whom were then household names for the clarity of their broadcasting voice. Drew Stevenson was the successful candidate. The auditioning process may have implied that all obstacles, financial and otherwise, had been resolved. They actually had been resolved, only for another one to suddenly appear. In discussions with the GPO it emerged that transmitting the commentaries would be more expensive than expected. At this late stage this could have put it all in jeopardy. However a spirit of compromise prevailed to the mutual satisfaction of each party. Talks took place in October with the resolution landing in November. Engineers then descended on Somerset Park to connect the necessary extensions to the landline. "The first relay will be on 28th November". This declaration was made in a tone of absolute certainty. It was devoid of disclaimers such as 'subject to' or 'hopefully'.

The inaugural match was a 'B' Division visit from Dundee United. Provost Adam Hart introduced the landline relay then Drew Stevenson proceeded to give what was described as a thrilling commentary. These initial broadcasts were made from a seat in the stand and, during the Dundee United match, Mr Stevenson had difficulty in shielding the microphone from the wind. From time to time he was assisted by Arthur Stanley. At half-time Harry Cattenach came on to voice his pleasure at the realisation of it all. Feedback was later sought from the hospital patients who had listened to the initial commentary. There was consensus that the excitement and the thrills had been expertly communicated. One elderly patient commented: "Ah widnae mind bein' in ma hoaspital bed every Setterday." It helped that Ayr United won 2-1. It became a popular facility with visually impaired fans who could listen from their seat at the match.

In addition to Drew Stevenson and Arthur Stanley, other early commentators to render fine service were George Hearton and Willie Shields. The latter became a legend of these commentaries. He did his first commentary in 1954 and continued for six decades. In time Stewart Clark would become another commentator of longstanding with more than fifty years of service. The facility got extended to cover the Biggart, the Ailsa and, from its opening in 1991, Ayr Hospital.

*The broadcasting studio in 2023.*

On 9th May, 1954, the Supporters' Association resumed the next phase of the wall separating Somerset Park from Walker's yard. It was again the remit of the Building Committee. The longer evenings were of great assistance. On a typical evening there would be a squad of volunteers working industriously to the accompaniment of a cement mixer whirring away. By the start of June 3,000 bricks had been laid on this phase of the work. Come the end of July the wall was complete from the railway end to a point opposite the half-time scoreboard. Sustained wet weather hampered the progress. It had been hoped to finish the final two-thirds by the start of the 1954/55 season. This would have been a high hope even if the weather had not been inclement. Drumming up volunteers was more difficult than it had been several years earlier and this too had an impact on the timescale. There was a degree of fan apathy created by the club's tenure in 'B' Division being too long. On a typical shift there would be about seven volunteers and maybe a couple of juveniles. It was no longer the army of volunteers of several years before. By the middle of October the wall was complete to half of its projected length. The foundation and base of the other half had already been laid and the material required to finish the job was already there. It dragged on for close to another year. Completion took place on the Sunday shift on 25th September, 1955. Rome wasn't built in a day and neither was the retaining wall running the entire length of Somerset Park's northern boundary. To put it concisely it was a magnificent piece of construction work. The Ayr United board agreed and the directors hatched a plan to set a commemoration plaque into the wall. Matt Pollock, in his capacity as club chairman, would carry out the unveiling ceremony. A wooden block and brass plaque was prepared and after a little deliberation the following wording was deemed to be suitable. "This wall was built and completed by voluntary effort by Ayr United Supporters' Association. October 1955." Alas the plaque did not appear. 1955/56 was a promotion season so it seems fair to attribute the oversight to all the excitement.

The large projects embarked upon by the Supporters' Association should, by now, have left this organisation exhausted financially and otherwise. Would there be enough reserves of money and willpower to set out on another big project? Yes of course there would. These people were possessed of great moral fibre.

In June 1958 plans were prepared for the construction of a broadcasting studio at Somerset Park. By late September the plans had been approved. The trustees of the Ayr Hospital Relay Fund had the responsibility of administering the project. Broadcasting while seated amongst spectators had disadvantages which were recognised. In the initial broadcast in 1953 Drew Stevenson had to juggle the microphone to shield it from the wind and there was the issue too of crowd noise and having to pass the microphone along when changing commentator. A further incentive for constructing the studio was the possibility of extending the facility to include general broadcasts of a non-football nature. The earmarked location was on top of the store adjoining the gymnasium i.e. in proximity to the corner arc at the railway end on the stand side. It would comprise a broadcasting room measuring 5 feet x 11 feet 7 inches and an equipment room measuring 7 feet 7½ inches  x 11 feet 7 inches. A striking feature was a 5 feet wide window angled at 45° in order to make it possible for commentators to see every part of the pitch from their vantage point. The pledge that there would be no delay in starting the work was fulfilled. On Monday, 6th October, 1958, it began. On the Saturday prior some funds were raised in the time-honoured manner. At the Ayr United versus Queen's Park game the collection tins were out and by this means £46 : 0s : 7d was raised. The Ayr United board contributed a cheque for £19 : 0s : 6d which may seem a random amount but there is an explanation. Older fans will recall that trial matches were held on the Saturday prior to the season starting. These matches were Ayr United versus Ayr United with a typical billing being Probables versus Possibles. The cost of entry was a matter of putting whatever you liked into a collection tin and the money collected in this way in 1958 was set aside and ultimately paid into the fund for construction of the studio. Such contributions at least made a dent in the overall cost. Somewhat vaguely the cost was estimated at "several hundred pounds".

*Gordon Lees. A longstanding committee member of the Supporters' Association.*

# AYR UNITED F.C.
## SUPPORTERS' ASSOCIATION

## SEASON 1959-60

**President:**
A. MAIN,
37 Springbank Road, Ayr.

**Vice-President:**
J. MUIR,
114 James   Campbell Road, Ayr.

**Secretary:**
W. McVEY,
Hillside, Kilkerran, Maybole.

**Minute Secretary:**
G. W. LEES,
20 Armour Drive, Ayr.

**Treasurer:**
J. C. STIRRAT,
3 Glenriddel Road, Ayr.

**Social Convener:**
Mrs. R. MARTIN,
28 George's Avenue, Ayr.

*Bank:* NATIONAL BANK OF SCOTLAND, LTD.

*All communications to be addressed to the Secretary.*

" Advertiser " Office, Ayr.

*1959/60 Supporters' Association membership card.*

Notwithstanding that raising finance was a big factor the plan was always going to succeed. The spirit and enthusiasm was boundless therefore Old Lady Somerset's broadcasting studio was duly delivered. It was opened on the Wednesday evening of 12<sup>th</sup> August, 1959, when Falkirk were at Ayr for a League Cup sectional tie. With due allowance for it being an early stage of the League Cup and it being in midweek, the crowd looked massive. Conservative estimates put it at 11,000. 1958/59 had been an all-conquering season in which Ayr United had made a rampant return to the First Division and even in the face of Second Division opposition in the League Cup the fans were happy to retrace their steps to Somerset Park. The studio was formally opened by Dean of Guild Adam Hart. Also in attendance at the opening were Supporters' Association chairman Harry Cattenach and secretary Gordon Lees. Mr J. Main represented the Board of Management for Southern Ayrshire Hospitals. James Frew represented Ayr United. From the luxurious precincts of the new studio three goals were reported in the first twenty minutes. They were scored by John Telfer (10), John White (11) – Falkirk and Peter Price (19). That's the way it finished, 2-1 to Ayr. John White was just two months away from a transfer to Spurs.

The 1950s comprised a decade in which the Ayr United Supporters' Association had been hugely kind to Old Lady Somerset. It has to be acknowledged, of course, that the whole broadcasting venture had been in the hands of the Relay Fund Trustees which, although an offshoot of the Supporters' Association, was nonetheless an independent body. With time ticking on the decade the Association donated £500 towards the cost of terracing improvements at Somerset Park in addition to equipping the gymnasium with medicine balls, skipping ropes, wall bars and a punch ball at a combined cost of £130. A relative prosperity had been generated since their provision of catering facilities within the ground.

*Chapter Seven*

# The Darkest Hour

Anyone brought up in the 1960s will testify that it was virtually mandatory to buy the *Sunday Post*. It was almost as if there was a law compelling it. The Fun Section would get detached from within the paper and handed to the children in the household, this being the part containing The Broons and Oor Wullie. However the grown-ups also enjoyed a read at it. Your writer's family complied with the convention but we purchased another newspaper along with the *Sunday Post*. That newspaper was the *Sunday Express*. On reading the edition dated 22nd November, 1964, it was immediately apparent that the expression 'Jings, crivvens, help ma Boab!' was more appropriate to that publication than its D.C. Thomson rival. The *Sunday Express* would not normally appeal to a child. On that particular Sunday I was precisely one week away from my twelfth birthday but the memory of the back page headline will never fade. Then, as now, it was customary to read the back page first.

The headline was:

AYR UNITED MAY QUIT

The sub heading was:

After 53 years a closedown looks imminent

53 years should have read 54 years but this was not a time for being pedantic. There followed a story illustrated with a photograph of a near deserted terracing at the match the day before – Ayr United 2 Montrose 1. As one who attended that match you may be told that the frugal attendance was not especially alarming. With the club anchored to the foot of the Second Division it had become normal. The following was written by the Sports Editor.

> "The future of Ayr United Football Club is in the balance. I understand that a move may be made very soon for a special meeting of the board to consider the situation and a motion may be tabled to wind up the club

voluntarily. If the club closed soon they (the directors) feel then that the sale of the ground, which is in an industrial area, would almost certainly be enough to clear up any outstanding deficit and permit shareholders to get their money back. The last club to leave the Scottish League were Leith Athletic – expelled by the League in 1953 after struggling to keep their head above water in Division 'C'. In 1953 they were expelled after failing to fulfil their league engagements. They played in the Scottish Cup in 1954 and were finally liquidated in 1955."

## SECOND DIVISION

**Ayr United 2 Montrose .. 1**
HALF-TIME 0—1

**Berwick ... 2 Raith Rov. 3**
HALF-TIME 2—2

**Brechin .... 1 Queen's Pk 4**
HALF-TIME 0—3

**Dumbarton 3 Cow'nb'th 0**
HALF-TIME 1—0

**Forfar Ath. 1 Alloa ....... 3**
HALF-TIME 1—1

**Hamilton . 2 Stranraer .. 2**
HALF-TIME 0—2

**Qn. of Sth 2 Albion Rov 1**
HALF-TIME 2—0

**Stenh'muir 1 Arbroath . 3**
HALF-TIME 1—0

**Stirling Alb 1 E.S. C'bank 4**
HALF-TIME 0—1

| | P. | W. | D. | L. | F. | A. | Pt |
|---|---|---|---|---|---|---|---|
| Stirling Albion | 17 | 12 | 3 | 2 | 41 | 16 | 27 |
| E.S. Clydebank | 18 | 11 | 4 | 3 | 35 | 16 | 26 |
| Hamilton Acas. | 15 | 8 | 5 | 2 | 31 | 20 | 21 |
| Arbroath | 16 | 8 | 5 | 3 | 30 | 17 | 21 |
| Queen's Park | 17 | 9 | 3 | 5 | 26 | 18 | 21 |
| Queen of South | 17 | 6 | 8 | 3 | 34 | 23 | 20 |
| East Fife | 14 | 8 | 1 | 5 | 33 | 31 | 17 |
| Berwick Rangers | 16 | 7 | 2 | 7 | 31 | 32 | 16 |
| Albion Rovers | 16 | 7 | 2 | 7 | 27 | 25 | 16 |
| Alloa | 17 | 5 | 5 | 7 | 31 | 41 | 14 |
| Stranraer | 17 | 4 | 6 | 7 | 31 | 41 | 14 |
| Raith Rovers | 18 | 4 | 6 | 8 | 28 | 35 | 14 |
| Brechin City | 18 | 5 | 4 | 9 | 28 | 41 | 14* |
| Forfar Athletic | 16 | 5 | 3 | 8 | 32 | 37 | 13 |
| Montrose | 16 | 4 | 4 | 8 | 38 | 44 | 12 |
| Stenhousemuir | 15 | 5 | 2 | 8 | 22 | 31 | 12 |
| Cowdenbeath | 16 | 3 | 6 | 7 | 20 | 29 | 12 |
| Dumbarton | 17 | 5 | 2 | 10 | 24 | 15 | 12 |
| Ayr United | 16 | 3 | 3 | 10 | 19 | 32 | 9 |

*The Second Division table at close of play on 21st November, 1964.*

The demise of Leith Athletic was irrelevant to Ayr United's situation but all else in the story was of huge relevance. It was not worded in a sensationalist tone and it raised a variation of nightmarish concerns. The unanswered questions were these. How close was it to the truth? What was the source of the story?

It was known that the board would be meeting on the Tuesday evening. Would the outcome allay or fuel the crisis? Especially chilling was the suggestion that the directors were considering a motion to voluntarily wind the club up. If the motion was to be tabled and approved Ayr United would cease to exist and Somerset Park would be sold off for industrial development in order to repay debts. In the two days pending the meeting the board remained silent. The suspense was terrifying to those who cared. Unfortunately too few of us did care, even locally. With the club foot of the pile in Scottish football's hierarchy the apathy was understandable and the major fear was that this level of disinterest would be shared by the board. After the meeting a statement was issued on behalf of the board by club secretary John Robertson, a measure considered necessary in view of "the unwelcomed press publicity". It read as follows.

"The directors having considered the financial position
with our advisers have decided that the club will carry on.
The length of time the club will be able to carry on depends
upon the support it receives from the public of Ayr and
district through the turnstiles and the Development Club."

In what was a crisis in the true sense of the word it was a very short statement yet it was long enough to contain a couple of frank confessions. The decision to carry on implied that winding the club up was considered to be an option. Yet perhaps more disturbing was the admission that the period of survival would be dependent on the efforts of the Development Club (an early day manifestation of the Ayr United lottery) and support through the turnstiles. Support through the turnstiles! Five seasons earlier Ayr United had beaten Rangers and Celtic away from home in the First Division. From personal testimony you may be told that in the Peter Price era Somerset Road was a sea of humanity ten to fifteen minutes before kick-off. Only the most foolhardy of motorists even attempted to meander their way through the crowds converging on Somerset Park. Also from personal testimony you may be told that in 1964 the situation was the polar opposite. Attendances were typically about 500. Note the word 'attendances'. It would be inappropriate to label such a small assembly of fans as a crowd. There seemed little prospect of the turnstile attendants getting any busier in the near future and the statement from the board implied that even if the club could eke out an existence for what remained of 1964 it would merely be a stay of execution until 1965 unless the lost fans would return. For some of us the question of returning did not apply. We continued to turn up on the sparsely populated terracing through thick and thin. Although mainly thin! There was no incentive for the lost fans to return with the club at the foot of the pile in the Scottish League. The glory days were a short memory away but might just as well have been in another century. In the immediate aftermath of the *Sunday Express* story three offers were made for striker Eddie Moore, all of which were rejected. It can reasonably be assumed that these offers were too meagre for consideration. A suitable analogy would be vultures picking at a corpse. There was speculation about a group of West of Scotland businessmen being prepared to launch a takeover. Media enquiries managed to solicit just enough detail to suggest that there was substance to the speculation but not enough detail to find out the identity of those involved. Although preserving their anonymity the group did leak that, in the event of a successful takeover bid, they would approach Ayr Town Council with a request to rent Dam Park if, through necessity, the sale of Somerset Park had to take place.

The first match after the explosive revelations was a league visit from East Fife. Did the plea for the return of the lost fans have any effect? It did not. Sacrificing the three shilling admission cost was an unlikely contingency based on sheer sentiment, especially on a wet and windy day. Only a winning team would have the desired effect. Ayr United 3 East Fife 0 was the score by the 21st minute but the strong wind was a key factor. A goal was conceded in the first minute of the second half and it ended 3-3. The team survived for a draw and the club survived for another week.

As if to compound the unease the next fixture was Stirling Albion away. This comprised top versus bottom and the result conformed with what might have been expected – Stirling Albion 5 Ayr United 0. History would show that this was Ayr United's last ever defeat at Annfield Park. The *Ayr Advertiser* report was commendably upbeat. It praised the team for playing well in phases of the game and bemoaned the injustice of a disallowed goal. A rallying call rounded it off.

"However black the financial situation is, in all fairness the stay away fans should realise that with a bigger support this side might produce better results."

The expression 'Catch 22' might have been made for Ayr United's plight in these closing weeks of 1964. Fans stayed away because of the results and the solution to getting better results was more fans! Yet no matter what was said the stark truth was that the air was rent with apathy.

Who, if anyone, was going to rescue Old Lady Somerset? Within days of the rout at Stirling the old adage that 'things could only get better' was turned on its head. Bobby Flavell turned up at the Tuesday night board meeting and resigned from his role as manager. Was he deserting a sinking ship or was his reason plausible? He ran a pub in his home town of Airdrie and he claimed that he could not do justice to both jobs. The status of Ayr United in 1964 was so low that the managerial job was of secondary importance to running a pub in Airdrie.

The day-by-day and week-by-week existence moved on to 12$^{th}$ December which saw a 3-0 win at home to Stenhousemuir. Those of us who were now deemed to be 'the few' witnessed an Eddie Moore hat-trick. A Cardiff City scout was in attendance. Now this was a club who would not be liable to make a derisory offer for our valuable asset. A £20,000 offer would have been phenomenal but, alas, no interest was declared. With board meetings now assuming more importance than the matches it may have been wondered whether any revelations would emanate from the next Tuesday get together. There was a revelation. Tom McCreath was the new manager. Bobby Flavell, his predecessor, had played for Scotland and at club level one of his clubs was Millionarios in the Colombian capital of Bogota. One of his team mates there was future Real Madrid great Alfredo di Stefano. In contrast Tom McCreath ran a joinery business in Maybole and had never played at senior level. After helping to run Kirkmichael Amateurs in his home village his next role in football was that of trainer to Ayr United reserves from August 1964 until being elevated to club manager on 15$^{th}$ December, 1964. Budget was clearly a factor in his appointment but, notwithstanding the need for financial prudence, the much craved success would eventually occur under his tenure.

On 2$^{nd}$ January, 1965, the league visit of Queen of the South drew an abnormally large crowd which reached 2,000. To put it into context it was an exceptional attendance in the circumstances. Reports were punctuated with positive expressions such as "just like old times" and "more atmosphere". This fixture came in the wake of three consecutive defeats and we entered it in bottom place in the bottom tier. Yet it could not be perceived that the public were now listening to the persistent rallying call to return. Vintage fans will tell you that crowds were artificially inflated at the New Year. People would turn up through custom despite seldom, if ever, going to matches at any other part of the year. There was a good case for some of them being tempted back. Eddie Moore scored twice in a 3-1 win and we moved off bottom place, albeit that Stenhousemuir sat one point behind with two games in hand.

*The saviours. Left to right: John Paton, Tom McGawn and Lewis Thow*

Beating Queen of the South was not the club's only positive result that weekend. Between the Saturday and the Sunday fruitful discussions occurred which probably saved the life of Old Lady Somerset. A new infusion of capital took place with the revelation (yes that word again!) that Tom McGawn had bought out the major shareholding of Matt Pollock. The transaction was mutually beneficial because Mr Pollock had already let it be known that, on his doctor's advice, he wished to relinquish the position of majority shareholder. Mr McGawn was not new to the board, having been a member for more than a year. These developments took place after a proposed takeover bid, from someone who was identified as Mr X, had fallen through. In terms of the actual identity the only clues were that this was a former senior player who was now a Glasgow businessman. In a candid piece of editorial in the match programme it was suggested that what was really needed was 10,000 Mr Xs to turn up at home games.

Tom McGawn's move was swiftly followed by yet more revelations at the Tuesday night board meeting. Two new directors had been co-opted to the board. They were Ayr garage proprietor Bob McCall and Prestwick businessman John Paton. Mr Paton had founded a radio and television business in Ayr and Prestwick. The business had recently been purchased by British Relay. These boardroom changes indicated a new lease of life for Ayr United and the stability guaranteed the immediate future of both the ground and the club.

*Bob McCall*

Could the magic be weaved into onfield performances? With Ally MacLeod now influential in a coaching capacity of course it could but not quite in the immediate term. Yet losing 2-1 at Alloa on 9ᵗʰ January might even have been termed an improvement when weighed against defeats of 7-2 and 5-1 at that ground in two of the previous three seasons. In the aftermath would there be any more revelations at the Tuesday night board meeting or could this overused word now be put to bed? It transpired that there were yet more major developments. At the meeting a letter was read out from club chairman and local butcher William Paterson. The letter announced his resignation as chairman of Ayr United and also from the board. His replacement as chairman was an obvious choice. Tom McGawn was, after all, the club's largest shareholder. It was also revealed that two more new directors had been co-opted to the board at the weekend. They were Lewis Thow, who was immediately installed as vice-chairman, and Malcolm McPhail. Mr Thow was a former Ayr United player and he was involved in the running of the family's local glazing business. Mr McPhail was a nephew of Bob McPhail, a former Rangers and Scotland player. In what appeared to be a packed agenda it was agreed at the meeting that the club would appoint a full time manager to the Development Club.

There was an unanticipated financial windfall from the Scottish Cup. At the time the draw was made it was suggested that the preliminary round tie away to Highland League Keith could be the most important match in Ayr United's history. The suggestion was based on winning the tie then being lucky enough to draw a big club. Whereas the lack of finance had threatened to kill the club at the time of the draw, that fear had been banished by 23ʳᵈ January when the game took place. Keith were beaten at Ayr in a Wednesday afternoon replay and in the first round proper Partick Thistle were the visitors at Somerset Park on 6ᵗʰ February. The crowd (and it truly was a crowd) amounted to 7,058 excluding the packed stand. Gratifyingly it was predominantly a home support. An unexpected 1-1 draw was, in terms of finance, prospectively a better result than a home win. The 7-1 defeat in the Firhill replay was sufferable when weighed against the now almost certain financial stability.

At the end of the 1964/65 season a second bottom finish meant the ignominy of having to apply for re-election to the Scottish League. One year hence the Second Division championship was won and Old Lady Somerset was again hosting First Division football. It gave credence to the ancient saying that the darkest hour is just before the dawn.

## Chapter Eight

# Let There Be Light

In October 1953 the Ayr United board stated that the club had no intention of experimenting with floodlights. The question was asked in response to a floodlit Kilmarnock versus Manchester United match on the 28th of that month. This was at a time when some Scottish clubs were starting to instal lights which were used solely in friendlies. When the installation of floodlights became more prolific it put Ayr United at a disadvantage. This was due to limited experience of floodlit football. There was evidence that the team displayed a tendency to crumble when, during an away game, the host club switched on the lights. There was ample substance to support the fact that this was happening. Let us consider the three away games Ayr United played in November 1959, all of which were league fixtures. 7th November – Celtic : With Ayr United leading 2-0 the gathering gloom caused the lights to be switched on. Within a short space of time it was 2-2 through goals in 61 and 67 minutes. Six minutes from the end Jim 'Tottie' McGhee won the game for Ayr when he scored directly from a corner-kick but that did not destroy the line of thought that the team had been disadvantaged. 21st November – Kilmarnock: With Ayr United missing Billy Elliott through injury since the 20th minute (no substitutes then) half-time was reached with the score at 0-0. The lights were switched on at half-time and Kilmarnock scored three minutes after the break. In a 2-0 defeat a further goal was conceded seven minutes from the end 28th November – St.Mirren : The *Ayr Advertiser* report went so far as to print this headline .

VETO FLOODLIGHT GAMES UNTIL SOMERSET PARK IS LIT UP

There was a clear transformation when the lights were switched on. From leading 3-2 the match was lost 4-3 with St.Mirren scoring in 79 and 80 minutes.

From a modern perspective it may be difficult to understand why there was an issue. Yet it has to be understood that floodlighting then and floodlighting now cannot be remotely compared for quality. The difference was night and day if you will pardon the intentional pun! In particular it was difficult to follow the highlights of a televised floodlit game back then. Viewers were left with the impression that midweek games were habitually played in a fog. Viewing these games in person had similar drawbacks, most notably that players cast numerous shadows. Some Ayr fans of that era will tell you that the difficulty was caused by goalkeeper Ian Hamilton wearing contact lenses and being dazzled by the lights as a consequence. Whether or not that was true cannot be substantiated on this page.

It is a fact that, at the end of season 1959/60, Ayr United, by virtue of our league position, qualified for Europe. It was an Anglo Scottish French tournament comprising eight clubs from France and four each from Scotland and England. The club had to step down because Somerset Park did not have floodlights. Our place was given to the lower placed Celtic who were drawn to play Sedan home and away. The case for floodlights at Somerset Park was strong and may well have been implemented sooner had not the club fallen from grace thereby rendering the expense prohibitive.

In the autumn of 1969 thoughts at last turned to the question of a floodlighting system for Somerset Park. It was the only First Division ground in Scotland without floodlights. Maybe now the question of expense could be addressed. Ayr United had just returned to the First Division and beaten Hibs 3-0 in the opening league fixture. A fortnight later Rangers were beaten at Ayr on the day the ground record was broken. Then came the epic League Cup semi-final and replay against Celtic. The team was playing well and the public not only knew it but responded to it. Home crowds were rising substantially. Yet the estimated cost was high and the question of financial viability for such a project had to be approached with a tinge of caution. There were training lights at varying intervals around the pitch but these were basic and could not be modified for match purposes. An idea was hatched by John Fergusson which was sensible in the extreme. Under his chairmanship a floodlight fund committee was formed. Enquiries had solicited the information that the estimated cost of the floodlighting would be £18,000. Estimates being estimates the eventual cost would spiral to £21,170. The aim of the committee was to defray the expense by raising £10,000. Discouragingly

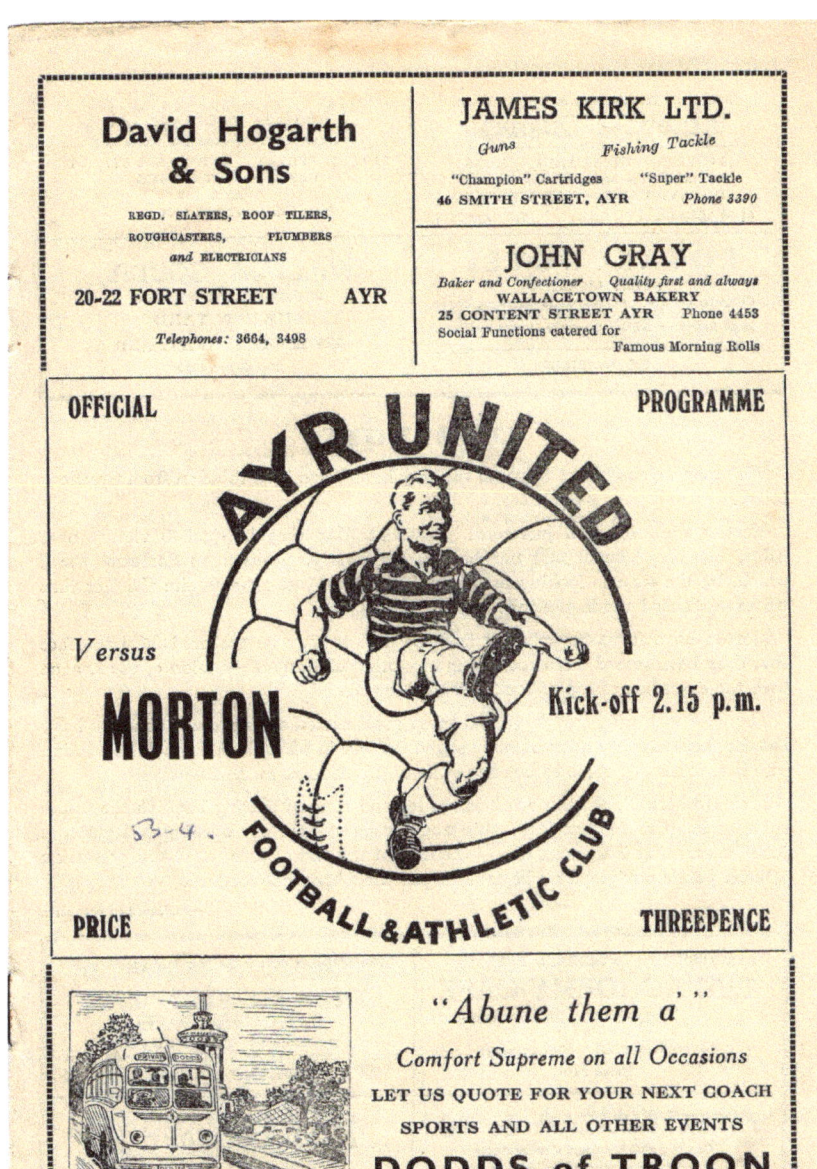

OFFICIAL            PROGRAMME

AYR UNITED

*Versus*

**MORTON**

Kick-off 2.15 p.m.

53-4.

FOOTBALL & ATHLETIC CLUB

PRICE            THREEPENCE

*Morton at home on 5th December, 1953. As indicated on the match programme cover it was not practical to have a 3pm kick-off in the dead of winter in the pre-floodlight years.*

93

they already knew that a previous attempt by another party had been aborted with just £700 raised. Undaunted the committee proceeded to smash their seemingly unachievable target. So how was it done?

The biggest event was a free gift auction on the night of 27th February, 1970. Many in the packed assembly could recall a similar Ayr United-related event on 23rd December, 1950. The similarity extended to the type of event and also to it being the same venue, Ayr Cattle Market. The 1970 event bore a further similarity to its predecessor in 1950 – the place was packed. All manner of goods and livestock got sold. The first item was a ten-week old west highland terrier with a pedigree. This cute little item sold for £15. The top price was the £101 paid by T. Murray & Sons for a Friesian bullock. £2,300 was made at the auction and this took the fund total to £10,500. A raffle on a huge scale had been taking place with the tickets selling for months. The last event at the free gift auction was the draw for the raffle. Individual donations had also helped bolster the fund. On the evening of 1st April a dance was held in the Bobby Jones with the proceeds going to the fund. No stone was left unturned in the efforts of the floodlight fund committee. Ultimately the sum raised was £12,201 : 14s : 11d. In July 1970 John Fergusson presented a cheque for precisely that amount to Ayr United chairman Bob McCall. It was a fantastic sum to raise in the period of well under a year. The committee put out the following press statement.

> "It is particularly gratifying that, as the fund closes, work on the erection of lights at Somerset Park is now in progress with every expectation of being completed in time for the commencement of the forthcoming season."

The first significant sign that the project would proceed had come in February 1970 when the Ayr United board accepted estimates for the various stages of the work. There was also confirmation that the work would begin and end that summer. On that basis the lights would be ready for the start of the 1970/71 season. The reality would prove different but it was a minor issue because floodlit matches do not occur in the summer anyway. The plan was for four pylons, one in each corner of the ground. Each would hold about thirteen bulbs.

Against the background of certainty that the work would go ahead, speculation began as to which club would be invited to hansel the lights. To speculate that it would be a top tier English club seemed reasonable but it was inconceivable that the inaugural match would take place as early as the dates being suggested in some national newspaper reports.

As Ally MacLeod explained: "What is the point in holding a floodlit match in the summer when it is still light at ten o'clock?" Mr MacLeod also said that he had a notion of inviting Liverpool or one of a number of top English clubs he had in mind but he was happy to defer an approach until nearer the time. The choice was entirely his rather than it being a board decision. Primarily he was team manager but he was possessed of a persuasive personality which allowed him to become supremely influential in all of the club's business. Nottingham Forest was another name to enter the mix. This was based on Alex Ingram having been sold to that club on 20th December, 1969.

*Ally MacLeod's supreme influence in the club's history was recognised on 26th February, 2022, when this memorial was unveiled in Tryfield Place.*

On the first day of June the work got underway. The first stage entailed a giant steam hammer being used to drive large metal tubes into the ground. These tubes were later filled with cement. With the height of the pylons exceeding 100 feet a very sound foundation was essential. The next phase involved erecting the pylons which were amongst the most modern in Britain. One of the last tasks would be the remit of the Electricity Board who would instal heavy duty cables. Those clubs who had installed their lights in the mid to late fifties would be left in the shadow, literally and metaphorically.

Four weeks before the commencement of the 1970/71 season the work was progressing steadily. It was expected that the four massive pylons would be delivered by the end of June and in place by the end of July thereby allowing the heavy duty cabling to be put in place in August. The lights being operational by some point in September seemed a realistic aspiration.

At the Annual General Meeting in August 1970 it was announced that Ayr United had made the largest ever profit to this point in history. For the year ending 31st March the profit was £49,444. Immediately upon the release of this news Bob McCall outlined his plans to improve spectator accommodation at Somerset Park. He stated: "I definitely have plans for a new stand opposite the existing one but the sort of building I visualise would cost at least £100,000. It would consist of two tiers, both with seating accommodation and a standing enclosure beneath." On his own admission such a grand plan was unlikely to materialise for a few years. However there was a Plan B which he did consider to be viable in the "not too distant future." The scheme he had in mind was to extend the stand in the direction of the gymnasium i.e. towards the railway end. He summed it up by saying: "These are just two plans we have been thinking about. We planned the installation of floodlights, the redecoration of the park and painted advertisements. The extension to the stand could be next in line." Ultimately a Plan C was implemented the following year, more of which later.

Although the forward thinking was praiseworthy in terms of ambition there was a more immediate priority. In fact it was more of a snag than a priority. The pylons had been expected to be delivered by the end of June but they arrived weeks later. Constituent parts had been sent in bits and pieces but some of the parts did not fit properly. On the positive side the erectors claimed that they could build a pylon in two days. It was a Meccano set on a colossal scale. By the second week in August two pylons were up but the plan had been for all four to be in place by this time. The erectors' claim to be able to build a pylon quickly was subject to the parts fitting. Many of the cables had now been laid and the bulbs had been delivered. However it was necessary to build a substation to supply power to the bulbs and that work had still to commence. Floodlighting bulbs are subject to the same vagaries as household bulbs in that they will eventually wear out. Those installed in 1970 lasted until September 1980 when they had to be replaced at a cost of £6,000.

*The match programme cover alludes to the official switch-on, albeit that the floodlights had been put to the test at reserve level.*

A further delay was caused by the pylon erectors going on holiday. They duly returned and by mid-September all four pylons were complete. They were most imposing and could be viewed for miles on the northern approaches to the town. By the start of October the lights had been linked to the source of power. The system was now operational but required to be tested before being used for a first team match. On 8th October, 1970, there was an opportunity for a test. This was a Thursday and we had a Scottish 2nd XI Cup first round tie against our Partick Thistle counterparts. The kick-off time was 5.30pm which was consistent with a match expected to finish in daylight. In the latter stages however the daylight started to fail rapidly and the floodlights were switched on for the remaining twelve minutes. Those of us who were there felt a sense of awe, albeit that this may sound ridiculous in the modern day. With five minutes to go the visitors drew level at 1-1 and this was perhaps fortuitous. The replay at Firhill also resulted in a draw and consequently the second replay was scheduled for Somerset Park on the night of 21st October. A 2nd X1 Cup first round second replay is ostensibly an inauspicious occasion yet this contest between the reserve teams of Ayr United and Partick Thistle was the first ever Somerset Park match to be floodlit in its entirety. The attendance was in the region of 2,000 for a game which would ordinarily have been witnessed by an attendance in the low hundreds. The great sensation of novelty superseded the 2-0 home win.

Fans were still mindful of the speculation about inviting a top tier English club to take part in a match to commemorate the switch-on of the lights. While negotiating with Newcastle United over the transfer of Phil McGovern an invitation was made and accepted. On the night of 18th November, 1970, a crowd of 7,500 watched the historic occasion. The result was Ayr United 2 Newcastle United 0.

In later years this was remembered as Somerset Park's first floodlit match due to a tendency to forget the actual first match in which Partick Thistle reserves were guests. Yet floodlit football, albeit rudimentary, had taken place in the town in an age well beyond living memory. As mentioned in Chapter One the first floodlit match in Ayr took place on Thursday, 7th November, 1878, when Ayr Academicals played Glasgow University at Springvale Park. The town's next experiment in floodlit football occurred on Thursday, 17th November, 1892, at Carrick Street Oval. This event was more successful in the context that it did not have to be abandoned. It comprised a five-a-side football competition as well as a cycling competition.

The lights erected in 1970 had a good life but they failed on one occasion. On 29$^{th}$ August, 1979, the place was plunged into darkness thereby causing the abandonment, in the 57$^{th}$ minute, of a second round League Cup tie against Hearts. The switchgear in the stand had burned out and it was beyond immediate repair. These lights were dismantled and replaced in the summer of 2011. This time there was no sensation of novelty and, in consequence, no glamour friendly against a major English club. The first match played under the new lights was a second round League Cup tie against Inverness Caledonian Thistle on the night of 24$^{th}$ August, 2011. The tie was won 1-0 and it was watched by a paltry attendance of 987. Floodlit football at Somerset Park had long since been taken for granted.

## Chapter Nine

# The Somerset Road End and the Turfing Dilemma

On Tuesday, 5th January, 1971, the Ayr Town Planning Committee had a meeting. Amongst the cases for consideration one in particular was intriguing. It was in relation to plans for the construction of a £12,000 covered enclosure at the east end of Somerset Park (better known as the Somerset Road end). Charles Eddie, the Ayr Burgh Surveyor, told the planning committee that the construction of the enclosure would not be affected by any possible legislation on safety at football grounds. He added that the building would simply be a frame and a roof. Mr Eddie was asked whether there were any planning objections to the proposed project. Humour is a rare commodity at planning meetings on a winter's night but his reply succeeded in injecting at least a little mirth. "No – except possibly from residents in adjacent houses who will no longer be able to see football matches for free." It was estimated that the enclosure would provide cover for about 5,000 spectators. The plans received approval. Ayr United's response to the outcome was clarified not by the chairman but by the all-influential Ally MacLeod. "The blueprints for the enclosure have been okayed but that is all. Nothing more will be done about it yet." In metaphorical terms this was interpreted as putting it on the back burner. The good news was therefore tempered by a warning to exercise patience.

It was not put on the back burner for long and consequently patience was not unduly taxed. By mid-May 1971 the foundation work had already begun. In suggesting that the work would be complete in good time for the start of the 1971/72 season there was no suggestion of wild optimism. The Burgh Surveyor had called it no more than a frame and a roof and that is precisely what it was. Nonetheless the ground was a hive of activity during that summer of 1971. While the enclosure was under construction major work was getting done to the pitch. At times in that previous season the turf was cutting up too easily and some games were contested in a mudbath. Your writer can recall hearing a visiting Falkirk fan venting an expletive-ridden rant about the turf (or lack of it!) and that was before the match had even started. The popular rumour at this time was that a broken underground drain was the cause of the problem. This was speculation in its wildest form. There were no drains beneath the grass. Traditionally the Somerset Park turf had a quality that would not have disgraced a bowling green. Alas that reputation was in tatters but no blame could be attached to the ground staff. The sub soil had to be renovated and this required the turf to be turned over. It was a huge undertaking involving 500 square yards in the centre of the pitch. Problem solved! It may have seemed so but the problem was far from solved. What was thought to be a permanent solution amounted to a very short term fix, more of which later.

*The Somerset Road enclosure shortly after completion but before it had been used on a match day.*

By the third week in July the enclosure was complete and ready for use in a pre-season friendly against Sunderland on 4th August. The link with Sunderland had been created when Dick Malone was sold to that club in October 1970. This friendly also saw the Black & White Shop opened for the first time. It was an iconic programme and souvenir shop located close to the half-time scoreboard on the north terrace. In mentioning that the inaugural match was a friendly it should be pointed out that it was this in name only. It was a bad-tempered 1-1 draw in which Gordon Harris, the Sunderland captain, was sent off. Sunderland's previous visit to Old Lady Somerset had taken place in 1896 and in 1888 they had played at Beresford Park, both games against the olden-day Ayr FC. A future visit was made in 1992.

*By 2023 the Somerset Road enclosure had lost none of its original character.*

At a board meeting on the evening of 19th August there was a shock. On the table was a letter of resignation from Bob McCall. He was not only stepping down as chairman but also as a director. His motive was pressure of business. Tom Murray, a former Provost of Maybole, stepped up to the chairmanship. Myles Callaghan became vice-chairman. The floodlights and the Somerset Road end enclosure were major projects implemented under Mr McCall's charge and he had already been forthcoming in mentioning his vision for other grand plans. His contribution to the evolution of Somerset Park had been immense. When the Annual General Meeting was conducted on 21st September there was more boardroom change in very contentious circumstances. Chairman Tom Murray was voted off the board by shareholders only to be re-elected minutes later in a special poll by his fellow directors. Then there was another poll with the result that two directors were voted off the board after they had been re-elected by shareholders. These directors were Lewis Thow and Malcolm McPhail, both of whom had injected substantial capital into Ayr United when the club was in danger of becoming extinct and the ground sold off for industrial development. There was an argument that the board had to be streamlined in 1971 because, with ten members, it was too big. Mr Thow was justly enraged and he commented: "I feel very bitter about this. So does Mr McPhail."

Ever since 1888 improvements to Somerset Park had been at the behest of ambitious committee men or directors. These were the people who possessed the sheer drive and business acumen required to oversee developments at the ground. Neither should we overlook the sterling efforts of willing volunteers this, of course, being a direct reference to the Supporters' Association in the 1950s. Team matters were of primary importance and in 1971 we were on the threshold of some halcyon years. In July Cutty Young had been sold to Coventry City and this was followed by a financial windfall when drawn in the same League Cup section as Celtic and Rangers. This was against the background of a part time wage bill, albeit that Ally MacLeod was a full time manager. It is an inescapable point that the board at this time began to follow a course of financial prudence. Ground improvements slowed other than the requirement for basic maintenance. Onfield prosperity did not translate to improving the surrounds. The railway end was terraced with railway sleepers. Crowd movement during a big match would leave them dislodged at all angles, sometimes raising clouds of dust in the process. Crush barriers were so flimsy that they were prone to buckling and there was no stepping on the northern exit onto Somerset Road thereby creating an almighty downhill scramble at the final whistle. It is a peculiar irony that safety measures became much tighter when there was a decline in spectator numbers.

*The enclosure's bleakest day. The Boxing Day storm in 1998.*

By January 1972 it was evident that there was a recurrence of a supposedly fixed problem. There was a bare patch in the centre of the pitch. The firm which carried out the turfing repairs in the summer of 1971 inspected the damage and agreed to sort it at no cost when the 1971/72 season was over. What could be fairer than remedial work at no cost? If only it had been that simple. Towards the end of April it became apparent that the required work would be extensive. This conclusion was drawn after turf consultants had been called in. It would be necessary to begin the work urgently as soon as the pitch was no longer required for playing or training purposes.

On 29th April the last home match was played. It was a 4-0 win over Partick Thistle in which Johnny Graham scored all four. Thereafter the playing surface was immediately prioritised and work started in early May. So what was the issue? In pursuit of the answer the club sought the advice of the Sports Turf Research Institute. These people were experts in the protection of surfaces at sporting venues and they had played a big part in the maintenance of the pitches at Hampden and Wembley. For the problems at hand there was no better consultancy to approach. The issues were succinctly clarified. No drains existed below the pitch, just twenty feet of sand with eight feet of loam above it. Loam is a soil type containing about 40% sand. Down through the years the top layer of loam had gelled which made it impervious to water. This was the process which had caused too much water saturation in the previous two seasons. By way of rectifying this the top four inches of the playing surface got lifted in preparation for sowing new seed. A camber was created in order to help clear away excess water. With a combination of over 2,000 tons of sand, peat, fertiliser and lime being used to form the top soil there was a confidence that this would be an effective resolution.

Within a fortnight of starting the process a fear emerged that the ground would not be available for use at the start of the 1972/73 season. These fears were soon to materialise. With the entire playing surface removed the pitch looked like a farmer's field. There was no chance that it would be sorted in time. In terms of cost it was vaguely stated that the project would set the club back "several thousand pounds".

On 24th May huge bags of grass seed got delivered and the sowing was carried out the next day. It was hoped that there would be some rain in the weeks ahead in order to give the grass a good chance of early growth. This was a classic case of being careful what you wish for. Several days later there was torrential rain which would have been fine had not the rain been accompanied by strong winds. In consequence the work done to this point had to be repeated.

The League Cup draw pitched Ayr United in a section with Rangers, St.Mirren and Clydebank, each to be played on a home and away basis. Neither of these games could be played at Somerset Park. A more realistic hope was that the ground would be playable for the league opener against Rangers on 2nd September. As for the League Cup where would 'home' be? It was tentatively arranged to host St.Mirren and Clydebank at Dam Park. The Rangers tie threw up two options. Both of the sectional ties against Rangers could be played at Ibrox or the 'home' match could be played at Rugby Park. When Ally MacLeod spoke people listened and this was his view on it: "There was a lot to be said financially for playing the game at Ibrox but in fairness to our supporters we wanted to keep the game as near to Ayr as possible". Kilmarnock readily offered the use of Rugby Park. This had to be ratified by the league committee and it duly was.

Whereas Dam Park was woefully short of capacity to accommodate a Rangers match there were no such shortcomings for a Saturday match against St.Mirren and a Wednesday evening match against Clydebank. Both were Second Division clubs and notwithstanding the fact that St.Mirren had the potential for a significant travelling support it was safe to assume that the capacity of the stadium would not even come close to being overtaxed.

On Tuesday, 30th May, Dam Park was inspected by a delegation of people including representatives of the police, representatives of Ayr Parks Department and an official of the sanitary inspector's department. At that week's meeting of the Ayr finance committee, director of parks Robert Wakefield said that Ayr United would be responsible for the policing of Dam Park and for manning the turnstiles. The Town Council would only have responsibility for providing a groundsman and marking the pitch. There was already a scale of charges in force for the use of Dam Park. It had been drawn up for amateur clubs but Mr Wakefield was straight to the point when he said that Ayr United would have to pay "rather more". The approximate capacity was put at 14,000 which may seem extraordinary in the present day. Back then there was more of a pack-them-in mentality. Rangers had won the European Cup Winners' Cup on 24th May and it would have been inconceivable to attempt to squeeze their vast support into the trim stadium on the banks of the River Ayr.

These arrangements had an adverse financial impact. The smaller stand at Dam Park was thought likely to accommodate only the club's season ticket holders. Income from the additional cost of watching from the stand would be lost.

With the match arrangements resolved thoughts turned to the re-seeding and the fervent hope that the seed would take quickly. There would be no pre-season friendly at home of course. This was a source of disappointment. In recent years there had been an air of anticipation about which English club would be visiting Old Lady Somerset. We had Halifax Town in 1968, Bolton Wanderers in 1969, Blackburn Rovers in 1970 and Sunderland in 1971. In 1972 the pre-season friendlies were at Cambridge and Stevenage.

Although the weather conditions were not entirely conducive the grass seed sown quickly took root. One week into June slivers of grass began to appear. The seed took more quickly on some parts than on others. This, according to people who knew about such matters, was a normal concept that could apply even to a small garden lawn.

Within days of the work starting Ayr United had entered a 21-year lease of training ground facilities at Craigie Park, just to the east of St.John's

Primary School on Whitletts Road. An annual rent of £390 was agreed. A clause was written in whereby there would be gaps in the lease at seven and fourteen years in order that the rent could be reviewed. The club would be responsible for maintenance. This initiative meant that Somerset Park would no longer be used for training purposes. Ayr United had been compelled to rip up full time contracts on the declaration of the Second World War. This was imposed on all member clubs by the Scottish Football Association. Here in 1972 the club was still part time and training took place on two nights per week. The arrangement at Craigie Park had the advantage of placing fewer demands on the new pitch.

As early as mid-July fears that the pitch would not be ready for the start of the league programme were receding. The transformation to a lush green surface was making steady progress. There was little prospect of having to open the league campaign against Rangers at Rugby Park. Would there be a miracle reprieve for the preceding League Cup ties? Certainly not. It would not have been worth the risk.

The situation was reminiscent of 1924 when the scale of work at Somerset Park necessitated playing home matches at Beresford Park in the early part of the season. On 12th August, 1972, there would have been veteran fans in the 6,500 Dam Park crowd who would have memories of that time. Failed attempts had been made to play at this location on a permanent basis and now it was Ayr United's temporary home. St.Mirren were beaten 2-1. Then, on the Wednesday evening of 23rd August, Clydebank were beaten 5-0. The supporters were enjoying life at Dam Park and so too were a lot of the patients just across the river in Ayr County Hospital. They could be seen watching these games from the hospital windows. It is tempting to suggest that what they witnessed was an aid to their recovery. By recourse to historical precedent it could have been argued that borrowing Rugby Park for the Rangers tie was simply the calling in of a favour. Kilmarnock had twice played a 'home' league fixture at Somerset Park. On 15th April, 1916, they beat Hearts 3-1 at Ayr, the reason for the switch being that Rugby Park was being used for a Cattle Show. On 26th January, 1946, Old Lady Somerset once more availed Kilmarnock of her home. In common with 1916 it was for a league fixture and this time they beat Partick Thistle 2-1. The reason given for the relocation was "the present state of Rugby Park." Alas this act of reciprocation did not produce an Ayr United win. This final match in the League Cup group saw Rangers win 2-1 but a new ruling meant that Ayr United would proceed in the competition as group runners-up. Merely three days later we met Rangers again and it was a home match in the true sense. The league opener marked a welcome return to a beautifully turfed Somerset Park. This homecoming was commemorated with a result of Ayr United 2 Rangers 1.

*30th August, 1972 – a 'home' game at Kilmarnock! The Ayr United players, left to right, are: Johnny Graham, Rikki Fleming, Phil McGovern and Stan Quinn.*

## Chapter Ten

# The Tryfield Place Vision

Up until 1976 a row of tenements ran the complete length of Tryfield Place. These tenements were immediately across the road from, and therefore in extremely close proximity to, the southern axis of Somerset Park. The demolition of these buildings together with the flattening of the former drying greens created a large expanse of spare ground. This ground fell under the ownership of Kyle and Carrick District Council and Ayr United were permitted to use it as a car park.

*Myles Callaghan*

During the first week of February 1980 chairman Myles Callaghan revealed that the club had been successful in acquiring the land and buildings at the junction of Tryfield Place and Back Hawkhill Avenue. To put it into context this was the triangular plot on the present day location of The Hub and its forecourt. The plan was to clear the area of the buildings and walls in order to create more room to manoeuvre at the turnstiles at the main gate. There was a reprieve for the cottage on that site. It was now the property of Ayr United and it was renovated in order to provide accommodation for the groundsman. In aesthetic terms the clearance plan was bland yet any initiative aimed at alleviating crowd congestion around the turnstiles hinted at a belief that there would be sizeable crowds to deal with. This was the second season since relegation from the Premier League yet this and other plans in the near future hinted strongly at the expectation of an early return. These soon-to-be-announced plans were massive.

The *Ayr Advertiser* dated 26th June, 1980, carried a front page story with the undernoted headline.

## SUPERSCHEME FOR SOMERSET

This was not an example of sensationalism. The scale of Ayr United's plans deserved any accolade heaped upon it. A press conference had been called for Thursday, 19th June. This was for the purpose of unveiling a project that was stunning. At an estimated cost of £500,000 the plan was to build a sports and social complex on ground occupied by the car park in Tryfield Place. Also included in the plans was an extension of the existing stand towards the west (railway end) to provide 600 more seats. Myles Callaghan told the assembled media representatives: "I am sure this will be of benefit to the people of Ayr and district and we have supporters very much in mind. There will be room here for them to hold meetings and functions. An application is being sent to the district council asking them to allow us to put in an offer for the purchase of the land. We are very hopeful that Kyle and Carrick District Council will look on our application favourably." He was quick to establish a co-relationship with onfield progress: "One is complementary to the other. There is no point in having an elaborate building on one hand and a poor team on the other. If we are to aim at the Premier League we have to have the surroundings and facilities to match."

Mr Callaghan touched on a potentially troublesome obstacle in mentioning that Ayr United did not own the land. Subject to negotiations running smoothly it was expected that work would start in about nine months time and the construction work would last for eighteen months. It was to be a T-shaped building extending to three floors and linked to the stand by a walkway above street level. The very large elephant in the room was finance. £½ million pounds! This was 1980. Mr Callaghan said: "I hope that, since it is intended to provide sports facilities for the town as well as the club, we will receive a substantial grant from the Sports Council."

*Myles Callaghan is the central figure surveying the plans for the superscheme. Team manager Willie McLean is far right.*

Plans had been drawn up by the Ayr firm of Cowie Torry and Partners. Ian McGill, a senior partner, proceeded to outline the scheme.

GROUND FLOOR

The gymnasium measuring 29m by 16m will occupy the leg of the T-shaped building and will be a multi-purpose unit. Left open, the gymnasium will be able to accommodate four badminton courts or an area where badminton, volleyball, indoor bowls, archery, hockey, six-a-side cricket or five-a-side football could be played. Divided by a third, the smaller section could be used for cricket practice and the larger area for sports like indoor bowls, archery, badminton or table tennis. Split in half, there could be two badminton courts and a general gymnasium area for activities such as keep fit or judo.

Adjacent to the gymnasium will be the entrance hall and changing rooms. It is possible that a sauna could be included in this section of the building. Also on the ground floor will be four squash courts – two underneath a glass-panelled lounge, one with its own gallery and a fourth which will be completely enclosed, ideal for beginners who might be intimidated by spectators.

FIRST FLOOR

Access to this and the top floor will be by lift or stairs. There will be an informal lounge with bar overlooking the gymnasium and two of the squash courts.

SECOND FLOOR

This will house a second, much larger lounge and bar capable of holding 440 people comfortably. There will be an adequate stage for cabaret artistes or a dance band and there will be committee rooms which can be used as changing accommodation. A kitchen will be used to provide food for functions.

STAND EXTENSION

Six hundred extra seats of the tip-up variety will be provided in the extension to the western end of the present stand. This will be linked with the sports and social complex by a passageway constructed above street level to allow vehicles to pass underneath. It is also intended to provide new changing rooms for the home and away teams under the new extension.

The presentation was very precise yet it did throw up some questions about the practicality of it all. It could not proceed on the mere hope of a Sports Council grant. Also the use of the earmarked land would cut down on the car parking capacity, albeit that the finished scheme would provide space for 200 cars. Most pertinently the ground was not Ayr United's to earmark. The council would be required to agree to the sale of it. It would need something more substantial than hopes to pull it all off yet with Myles Callaghan as the club chairman there had to be a chance. He had shown a flair for business by building up an expanding construction firm and he was devoted to the Ayr United cause.

During the first week of September 1980 there was a tentative step forward. Kyle and Carrick District Council agreed that their estates section should begin negotiations with Ayr United with a view to selling the required site. The club's legal representatives would handle the talks. Step one would be for the district council to approve the sale of the land at Tryfield Place. This would then put Ayr United in a position to submit the plans for approval by the council's planning and building control committee. It was one step in a potential marathon. Yet the potential fell a long way from realisation. The scheme perished on several rocks. It was expensive, problematical and based on an assumption of early promotion to the Premier League. With two automatic promotion places being available promotion was a realistic contingency for much of the season. Much of the season but not it all! Hope was extinguished during March 1981 and the club saw the season out by slumping to an ignominious final position of sixth. Yet the notion of the grand scheme was not completely extinguished at this time. It remained, as the saying goes, on the back burner. In February 1989 the club announced that there would be a feasibility study into the possibility of full time football from the start of the following season. Having been part time since 1939 this was a bold statement of intent. George Smith, the chairman, said: "If, because of full time football, we have to delay the social club, I hope the fans would understand." The plan for full time football did get implemented in 1989 but in the same year all hopes of the superscheme died a death when the foundations were laid for the construction of the Centrum Arena at Prestwick Toll, albeit that delays in construction deferred the opening until 1996. In terms of the facilities there was an overlap with those that had appeared on the plans for Tryfield Place. There was a modicum of irony that the logo on the Ayr United shirt in 1989/90 and 1990/91 bore the advertising logo Centrum.

The fine detail of the substantial background work was rendered irrelevant and the notion of a superscheme did not resurrect itself. It was therefore consigned to history.

*Chapter Eleven*

# The Segregation Fence

*November 1980. The catalyst for debate on the fencing issue.*

On the evening of 5th November, 1980, Dundee were at Ayr for the first leg of a League Cup semi-final. Even with due allowance for the fact that both clubs were in the second tier the attendance of 6,801 was modest. In reaching this stage Ayr United had beaten two teams from the Premier League. In turn those were Morton and Hearts. The Hearts tie had been a rout which ended in a 7-2 aggregate win. Knocking out Hibs was also noteworthy even although the opposition also had second tier status. Above all the Dundee tie was an opportunity to attain a level the club had never reached to this point of history – a national final, albeit that there would be a second leg in a fortnight. In retrospect the tie was deserving of a much bigger audience. Here in 1980 that dream of reaching a final did not materialise yet the impact created by the sub-7,000 crowd on that night had large ramifications.

Younger supporters will now be appraised of a long ago Somerset Park tradition which was vaguely tribal in its nature. As mentioned in a previous chapter, the turnstile which operated to charge extra admission to the railway end was decommissioned in November 1963. This allowed free movement within three sides of the ground. A large number of supporters, of whom your writer was one, would stand behind the goal the team was shooting towards then change ends at half-time. This involved a guessing game before the toss-up. Which way would the team be shooting in the first half? A wrong guess entailed hasty movement to the other end. At half-time this custom had the potential to get seriously messy. During this migration along the foot of the north terrace it was commonplace to meet opposition fans doing the same thing in the opposite direction. Football supporters do not have a reputation for exchanging pleasantries. Verbal exchanges were less than tender and, almost always, the conflict would end at that.

*5th November, 1980. The four policemen in the photograph are having a peek at Robert Connor's late equaliser. There was no reason not to. All of the crowd disorder took place at half-time.*

On the night of the Dundee match, half-time saw an army of home supporters decamp from the railway end at half-time whereupon visiting supporters set out on the reverse journey. The Dundee support went by the most direct route – across the pitch! It could have been argued that this was a conscious effort to avoid confrontation by effectively bypassing the oncoming Ayr support. Yet their movement down the field was marked by a high degree of revelry on their part. It just had to be an act of mischief.

In the aftermath the Ayr United board was quick to respond. Italian-style fencing, designed to keep fans off the pitch, was mentioned as a possibility. Whether deemed to be a radical measure or not, there was a chance that the club might not even have a say in the matter. The subject had been under consideration for six months due to the onfield fighting at Hampden at the end of the Scottish Cup final between Celtic and Rangers. A proposal came from Chief Constable Patrick Hamill of Strathclyde Police. He had already sent a letter to Strathclyde Regional Council to ask that every general safety certificate issued to clubs under the Safety of Sports Ground Act be amended to include a requirement to erect perimeter fencing. The grounds in Strathclyde designated under the Act were those belonging to Queen's Park, Rangers, Celtic, Partick Thistle, Motherwell, St.Mirren, Morton, Kilmarnock, Ayr United, Clydebank and Airdrie. Ten of the eleven clubs were either in the Premier League already or had recently been there. The obvious reason for the inclusion of Queen's Park was their ownership of Hampden.

What happened at Somerset Park had the effect of rekindling attempts at some kind of action. The scenes prompted councillor James Burns, Strathclyde Region's vice-convenor and chairman of the region's general purposes committee, to say that a working party on the safety of sports grounds, involving police, fire, architectural and administration departments, would now prepare a detailed report on precisely what was involved. Somewhat vaguely the timescale for submitting the report would be "as soon as possible."

> one another. None of us wish to see the day when "Killie" supporters enter one end of the ground and Ayr fans the other—may that day never dawn.

*The editorial in the Ayr United match programme dated 24th September, 1960, viewed segregation with a sense of dread. Two decades were to pass before the day dawned.*

A glaring contradiction was that the issue under consideration was fencing the fans in yet a riot at Hampden was the catalyst for the debate and that was the only one of the eleven designated grounds that now had such fencing. On a national level Frank McElhone had made recommendations on this even prior to 1980. He had been the Under-Secretary of State for Scotland between 1975 and 1979. His remit included sport and his recommendations were aimed at "protection for players, officials and the pitches" by way of "fencing of not less than 1.8 metres high against spectator invasion." There was a proviso that "the fencing would have access points to allow the evacuation of spectators in an emergency." The points raised by Mr McElhone were now being seriously considered by Strathclyde Regional Council.

Fencing was not a new topic of conversation for the Ayr United board. Regular meetings were held with local police representatives and the subject had been broached. However when the Minister for Sport, Hector Monro, entered the fray some contentious dialogue caused a rift between Central Government, the Regional Council, the Scottish Football Association and the Scottish League. If only those Dundee fans had not trespassed on Old Lady Somerset's sacred turf!

In relation to the pitch incursion and its potential consequences Mr Monro said: "I do not see any immediate change in the Safety of Sports Grounds Act. Any changes would require Home Office approval and I personally do not feel that further financial burdens should be imposed on the clubs." The requirement for Home Office approval was at odds with the aforementioned James Burns of Strathclyde Regional Council. He said: "As far as I am concerned we have the power as the licensing authority to insist on fencing without Parliamentary approval. I am in no doubt that it is quite proper for us to do this." This left a situation in which the regional council concurred with the recommendations of the Chief Constable but central Government was of an opposing view and there were conflicting claims on who had the authority to decide. Ernie Walker, secretary of the Scottish Football Association, expressed his displeasure. "If the regional council and the Chief Constable have views on the fencing of grounds I would have hoped that they had spoken to us about that." Jim Farry, secretary of the Scottish League, was similarly minded. "We obviously have certain views on the matter but we were not consulted."

Then, as now, no one had the gift of prophecy. What happened at Hillsborough in 1989 would starkly illustrate the detriment of high perimeter fencing. The Ayr United board gave the idea scant consideration in 1980 and did not involve itself in the brouhaha the topic had caused in the outside world.

Within three weeks of the Dundee visit Myles Callaghan announced that the club would be taking remedial action of another type. The *Ayr Advertiser* carried this headline.

SEGREGATION AT SOMERSET

When the news broke that there would be a segregation fence at Somerset Park there were no 'ifs', 'buts' or 'maybes'. There was no mention of consultations. Nothing was ambiguous. The project was announced with commendable decisiveness. When reminiscing on the pre-segregation years some fans are apt to expound the view that rival supporters would stand on the terraces side by side and there was never any trouble. Lamentably it has to be said that there actually was trouble, albeit occasional rather than regular. Goal scoring was a potential flashpoint as were controversial incidents on the field. Flare-ups even occurred through a stray remark. At the New Year a blind eye was cast towards bags of alcohol being carried in. An Ayrshire derby with no segregation and alcohol in the mix! Rugby fans will tell you that such a scenario would be perfectly harmonious in their sport. In an ideal world it would have been harmonious at the football too. Alas it was not an ideal world.

Myles Callaghan habitually hinted at a quick return to the Premier League when talking about developments at the ground and he was true to form with this statement. "This work would have to be done if we go into the Premier League but after what happened in the League Cup tie it will have to be brought forward." Mr Callaghan's ambition was far from wayward. To this point of the season we had beaten three Premier League teams on their own ground. The season had opened with a win over Celtic at Celtic Park in the Drybrough Cup and, as previously mentioned, two Premier League clubs were beaten in the League Cup with an Ayr United win in the away leg in each case. Moreover the opening league fixture had brought a result reading Ayr United 5 Motherwell 0. This team had the capability to go the distance and it had developed into a dogfight with Hibs, Raith Rovers and Dundee. That the Premier League aspiration did not materialise was not an indication that proceeding with the construction of the segregation fence was a folly. Behavioural patterns alone dictated the necessity.

The plan was to divide the ground into two sections with the home support retaining about 60% of the available space. It would be built in the proximity of the half-time scoreboard and visiting fans would be housed at the railway end. One point had still to be decided upon. The board had still to ponder whether to build two fences in order to separate the rival fans with a no-man's land. After consideration this was the option exercised. Today people will talk about the segregation fence or its more popular title of the seggy fence. With apologies for extreme pedantry we should be talking about the seggy fences.

The construction work was deferred until March 1981. Hibs were due at Ayr on the 28th of that month and the last of the work was completed in neat time for that fixture. With a few days to spare the fences were secured by concrete and ready for use. It was an irony that the measure had been prompted by a likelihood of returning to the Premier League. Hibs won 1-0 and any lingering hope of promotion was as good as extinguished on the day segregation was introduced to Somerset Park. There was a further degree of anti climax. Heavy rain enforced the fans to stand in the enclosures at the respective ends. The north terrace was therefore close to being deserted and very few fans risked getting drenched for the sake of a close-up view of the new barriers. Even those few who dared had no more than a quick inspection. Out on the pitch the turf cut up badly and the gluepot conditions made a mockery of the returfing operation in 1972.

*The case for segregation is encapsulated in this photograph from Partick Thistle's visit on 29th September, 1984.*

*Chapter Twelve*

# The Family Stand

*George Smith*

In January 1989 news emerged that the construction of a Family Stand would be financially viable. With an estimated cost of £150,000 there was an assurance that the Football Ground Improvements Trust would give a 70% grant. The source of that money was national football pools and it was part of a £1 million package to help Scottish clubs. On the assumption that planning permission would be granted it was to be built as an extension towards the Somerset Road end of the existing stand with work taking place in the next close season. This was contrary to the discussions about a stand extension in both 1970 and 1980 when the proposed concept was to extend towards the railway end. The seating capacity would be around 400 and it would be reserved for children and parents. In addition a covered area for the disabled would be built underneath the stand extension together with new toilets. At this stage it was being spoken about in relatively tentative terms. That all changed by the third week in March when Barr Construction started the work. The proposal was becoming an actuality rather than just an architect's plan. On Sunday, 30th July, the club held an Open Day and this was the first opportunity for the public to view the extension close up. The first match after its completion came two days later. It was a friendly against Dundee United. A crowd of 2,442 saw a 2-0 defeat.

Club chairman George Smith was rightly proud of this enhancement to the ground. In a statement he said:

> "The face of Somerset Park has changed with the building of the new Family Stand. We realise that the lifeblood of the game of football is in the hands of our young fans and this new facility will only encourage the family support. It is hoped that the new stand is only the first phase of spectator facility improvements as we look ahead into the 1990s and beyond. All this can only be achieved with the loyalty of the club support, of which Ayr United can be justly proud. We keenly look forward to the challenges of the future that, with a team effort from everyone who has Ayr United's interests at heart, will see the club grow to greater things."

Note the recurring theme whereby ground improvements, once implemented, get qualified by a hope that the works are the first in a phase of future development. Historical precedent had already shown that such hopes were dependent on the future prosperity of Ayr United. Finance was the key and the completion of this work in 1989 coincided with the club offering players full time contracts for the first time since 1939. Here we have another recurring theme in that this initiative was considered necessary to get the club back into the Premier League. The board's logic was that fitness and coaching could improve and consequently attendances would rise with the success. Relegation to the third tier had only been avoided in the penultimate league fixture of 1988/89 therefore promotion in the near future was an unlikely, but meritorious, contingency. Yet regardless of speculation about onfield matters we could be sure that the cost of full time football would rail against further enhancements to the ground in the immediate term.

*In 1989 the Family Stand extension (far end of photograph) took the structure closer to Archibald Leitch's vision of seated accommodation running the full length of Tryfield Place.*

With the season barely underway the Family Stand became the subject of criticism. A story broke that forty of the seats might never be used because a safety barrier at the front hindered the view from the front row seats. George Smith said that the barrier had been installed on the insistence of Kyle and Carrick District's planning department. A spokesman for Barr Construction emphasised that the extension had been built in accordance with national regulations. The club insisted that tickets would not be sold for seats with a restricted view. A reader's letter in the *Ayrshire Post* did not hold back.

> "The recent revelations concerning the farce of the Family Stand only underlines the incompetence of those in charge at Somerset Park. Might I suggest that the Directors' Box be relocated to the stand extension – it's apparent that they can't see what's going on around them anyway, so they won't be inconvenienced by being in this (black and) white elephant. Hopefully someone from the Football Grounds Improvement Trust will have read all about it and will have the good sense to withhold payment."

Such a viewpoint was reflective of the dissent which had grown within the fanbase. In the opening league fixture of the season a 3-1 defeat had been suffered against Albion Rovers, this match being played at Airdrie's Broomfield Park due to redevelopment work at Cliftonhill Park. The performance went down badly with the travelling support. The reintroduction of full time football after fifty years had degenerated into a shambles and the prevailing mood festered a willingness to hit out at the club in any way possible. Defeat to Albion Rovers had triggered a shoal of newspaper letters. The observation that the season was young did not wash. On a personal basis I too wrote a scathing piece on the Albion Rovers shambles – in the official programme. No one was vigilant enough to censor it and it resulted in a phone call from Helen Nelson (Ally MacLeod's secretary) saying that the directors wished to speak to me before the next home match. That meeting was convivial, most especially the boardroom hospitality. Incidentally this wasn't the only 'we need to speak to you' meeting over the years. The point being made here is that some of the comments that were critical of the Family Stand were born out of frustration at what was happening on the field. How restricted was the restricted view? Not very is the answer. The barrier was constructed of railings and, even with the admission that viewing a match through railings is not wholly satisfactory, it was still possible to view the action over the barrier. To put it into context no complaints have been made about restricted viewing in the intervening years.

*This 1977 photograph is conspicuous by the absence of the Family Stand. Look closely and you will see a chimney. At the time of its removal Somerset Park was the only league ground in Scotland and England still to have a chimney.*

In August 1989 Somerset Park became impacted by new regulations imposed in the wake of the Hillsborough disaster which had occurred in April. At the Liverpool versus Nottingham Forest FA Cup semi-final ninety-seven fatalities occurred as a result of crushing on that afternoon at Sheffield. In the wake of that disaster clubs were now being instructed to lower the capacity for their standing areas by 15%. In 1988/89 the capacity of Somerset Park was set at 18,500. It was now being dropped to 15,873. The breakdown was: Stand 1,200 : Family Stand 393 : Stand Enclosure 850 : Terracing 13,430. On that basis Strathclyde Regional Council issued a safety certificate. With each passing year the club's connection with the Premier League was becoming ever more tenuous. By 1989 we had been missing from the top tier for eleven years. Hopes for a return were precisely that. Hopes! Albeit that the Family Stand was a favourable enhancement it was clear that nothing less than a big cup draw would test the capacity. On 6th February, 1993, we had a Scottish Cup visit from Rangers by which time the limit had been further reduced to 13,918. Precisely that number of tickets got sold although only 13,176 were used. Beyond doubt there would never be a threat of getting near to Old Lady Somerset's record number of visitors. On 13th September, 1969, 25,225 paid for entry to our league victory over Rangers, this number being supplemented by the undocumented number who gained entry by illegal means.

*On 13th September, 1969, Old Lady Somerset experienced her busiest ever day for visitors. The result was Ayr United 2 Rangers 1. Davy Stewart is the goalkeeper under the watchful eye of Dougie Mitchell.*

## Chapter Thirteen

# The Hospitality Boxes

At a time when the club was exploring all feasible income streams a plan was hatched to construct five hospitality boxes and a function suite at the back of the north terrace. Corporate hospitality had a most certain potential for financial reward in addition to letting the facility out for functions and meetings. The plans were drawn up and submitted to the planning department of Kyle and Carrick District Council. In May 1995 came news that the council had deferred a decision. Bill Barr, who was now the club chairman, expressed the hope that it was nothing more than a temporary setback. His hope was fulfilled and Barr Construction began work on it that summer. Relegation to the third tier had just occurred and in consequence there had been a diminution in gate receipts. There was a confidence that this project would comprise the goose that would lay the golden eggs.

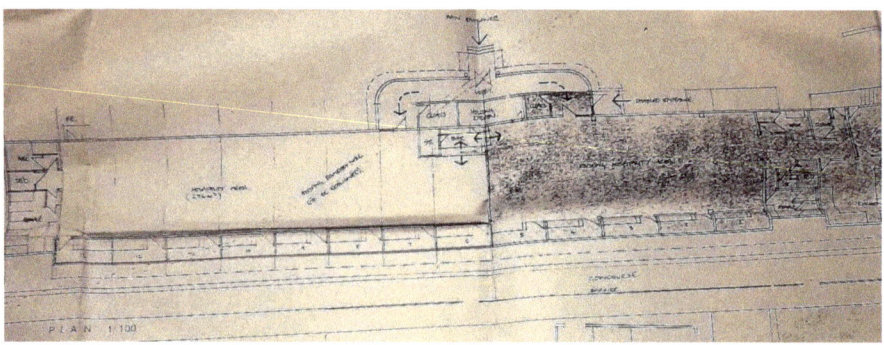

*This unimplemented plan, dated August 1995, would have made provision to extend the number of hospitality boxes to thirteen.*

On Sunday, 2nd July, 1995, an event advertised as the Ayr Carnival was held at Somerset Park. This afforded the public a glimpse of the partially completed structure. A pre-season friendly against Hartlepool United on the Friday evening of 28th July ostensibly showed the construction work to be finished but the interior had still to be fitted out. There was provision for vehicular and pedestrian access from Somerset Road and the finished work was really a joy to behold. Access was gained via the rear of the building with suitable provision made for wheelchair entry. On passing through the door a lobby area was entered with cloakroom provision. Thereafter entry was gained to the function suite containing a bar and a dance floor with an appropriate black and white chequered design. Quite obviously there was toilet provision in addition to a kitchen area. A storage room and a cleaner's room also got constructed. Plans dated August 1995 indicated the proposal of an extended scheme from five hospitality boxes to thirteen and with provision for even more function space. Further plans dated September 1995 showed a proposed stand with a seating capacity of 3,060. It was to be situated on the site of the north terrace and would extend from the front of the hospitality boxes down to pitch level. The outcome was the status quo of five boxes and the retention of the terracing.

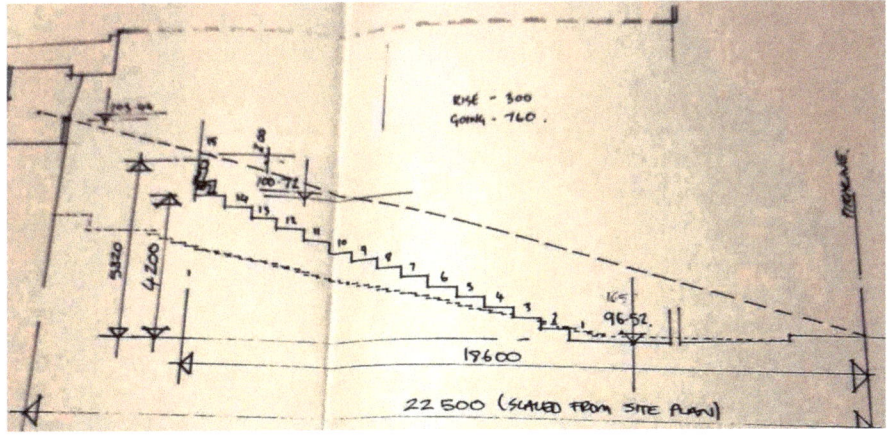

*This is a preliminary sketch dated September 1995. It shows the side elevation of a proposed stand with 3,060 seats. If implemented it would have been situated in front of the hospitality boxes which were then new.*

*The hospitality boxes prior to making way for renovations.*

In February 2011 the generically named function suite got renamed the Ally MacLeod suite. This occurred at a time when the *Ayrshire Post* announced that they would be sponsoring the facility. Sports Editor Mike Wilson initiated a scheme which fired the imagination of the fans. He publicised the names of twelve club legends who had played under Ally MacLeod's managership. The public had then to vote for their favourite player on the list and the top five would have a hospitality box named after them. Eleven of the twelve played in the same team. This was the team from 1969/70 which, even today, people can rhyme off effortlessly. These players were Davy Stewart, Dick Malone, John Murphy, Rikki Fleming, Stan Quinn, Dougie Mitchell, Cutty Young, Jacky Ferguson, Alex Ingram, Davy McCulloch and Bobby Rough. The odd player out was Henry Templeton from two decades later.

Cutty Young, Stan Quinn, Henry Templeton, Davy Stewart and John Murphy were the winning names. On 24th September, 2011, prior to a home match against Queen of the South, the Ally MacLeod Suite was formally opened by his wife Faye. With one exception the players whom the boxes were being named after were in attendance. It was unfortunate that John Murphy had work commitments. Commercial director Hugh Cameron welcomed the guests and there was a celebratory lunch. Vice-chairman Alex Ingram, who was Ally's first ever signing, gave a speech in which he reminisced about working under the great man. Fan John Dalton conducted a speech on the careers of the chosen five. Mrs MacLeod then unveiled both a plaque and a painting of Ally by local artist Richard Macdonald. The formalities were then completed when the club legends cut the ribbons to declare the respective boxes officially open.

Eventually the function suite was pressed into a totally unconventional use. Covid 19 created a premature end to the 2019/20 season. When football did resume for the 2020/21 campaign there was an air of surreality because no paying spectators were permitted. Deserted grounds and watching on a stream made for a very unsatisfactory experience but public health had quite correctly to be prioritised. Social distancing procedures had to be adhered to as rigidly as possible therefore the Ally MacLeod Suite got requisitioned as a visitors' dressing room. Watching a team clambering down the steps of the north terrace in order to take the field was indeed an odd sight. Simultaneously the home team emerged from the conventional route on the other side of the ground. The first home match of 2021/22 (versus Edinburgh City in the League Cup) had a very slight relaxation with a restricted capacity of 500. This 500 limit recurred between December and January for our home league fixtures against Raith Rovers, Arbroath and Morton. These mid-season restrictions, albeit temporary, proved that the health threat still lurked and it was an endorsement of the decision to use the Ally MacLeod Suite for changing facilities for the complete season. For season 2022/23 normal service was resumed when the viewing boxes were once more in use and the function suite was again used for a purpose not involving the clatter of muddy boots and sweaty shirts.

## Chapter Fourteen

# Heathfield – Attempt Number One

At an Ayr United Annual General Meeting the author was present when chairman Bill Barr fielded a question from a disgruntled shareholder about the inadequate state of the toilets. A meek apology might have been anticipated together with an assurance that matters would be rectified. However in a candid response Mr Barr said that there would be no upgrading and that his intention was to see Somerset Park bulldozed. He dramatically emphasised the point by putting his fists together and pushing them forward in a bulldozing motion. Most people reading this will have a deep love of Somerset Park and you may think that the thought of flattening the place was most callous. On the contrary. Bill Barr considered that relocation was best for the club. He had been chairman since October 1994 and he was as much a fan of Ayr United as those of us who were terracing dwellers.

In March 1996 he made a twin pledge. The first pledge was that the club would strive towards financial recovery and the second pledge was that stadium plans would be revealed once the club's league status was assured. Assuring league status was a euphemism for avoiding relegation to the fourth tier. For the financial year ending 30th June, 1995, the losses were a record in the history of the club. Losing £303,878 equated to about £6,000 per week. The accumulative debt to that date was almost £1.4 million. These losses were reported at the Annual General Meeting on 15th April, 1996, by which time the team had ascended to fifth thereby banishing any threat of the drop. How was it possible to square the finances with the twin pledge made several weeks earlier? Mr Barr said:

> "These accounts take into affect a lot of wage arrangements which were in force before I became chairman. Since then we have restructured the whole finances of the playing side and turned round the club's commercial side. Our figures for the six months up to last Christmas are very much healthier".

It helped too that York City had paid £75,000 for John Sharples three weeks before the Annual General Meeting and that Franck Rolling had gone to Leicester City for £100,000 in the intervening period since the year covered by the 'worst ever' balance sheet. In response to the stadium matter he merely said that three or four options were being considered.

In June 1996 the stadium speculation recurred when Mr Barr issued the following update.

"If the club receives the formidable support next season, which I think it now deserves, then there is no reason to prevent us from playing in a much improved stadium in the future. Such a decision on expenditure for a club like ourselves is perhaps made once in fifty years and I am sure that genuine supporters and shareholders understand that it is vital that we make the right decision."

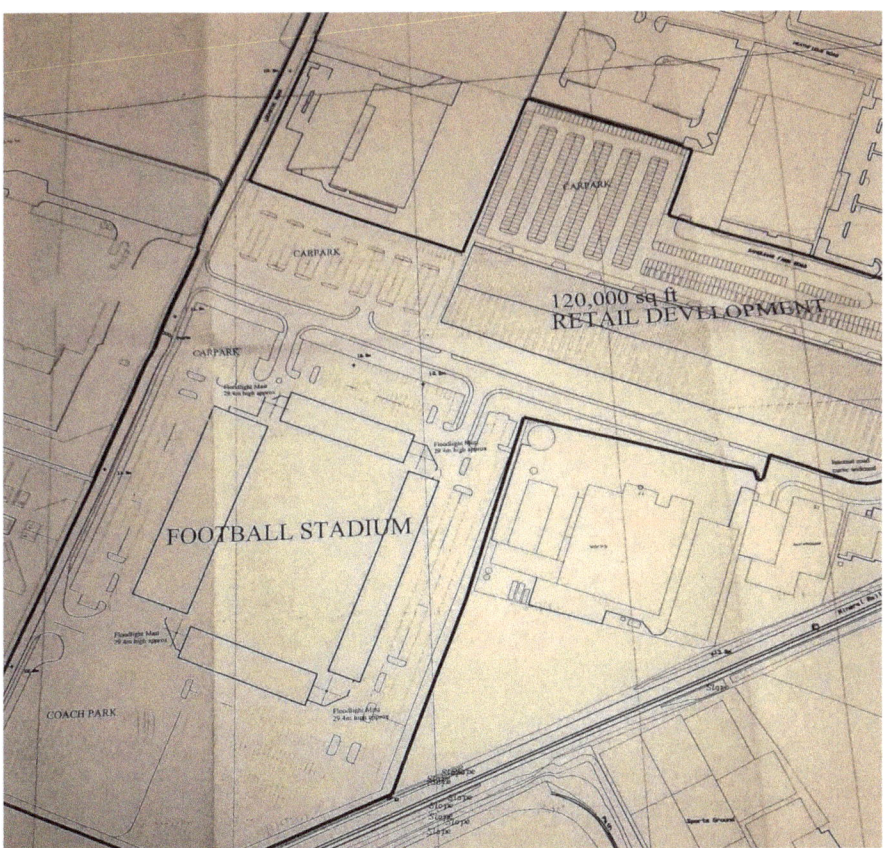

*This plan showing the new stadium and associated retail element is dated November 1998. Despite a tsunami of public support it did not progress from the drawing board.*

Barr Construction was on the brink of becoming prolific in the construction of new football stadia throughout the United Kingdom. With mind numbing naivety people would ask why Bill Barr could build stadia for other clubs but not for his own club. His response was: "I wish these people would be in possession of all the facts because my colleagues and myself have spent a great deal of time considering the matter". This reference to people not being in possession of the facts alluded to the complexities of planning legislation. Oh for the simplicity of 1888 when the process was dismantle, cart away, relocate and rebuild.

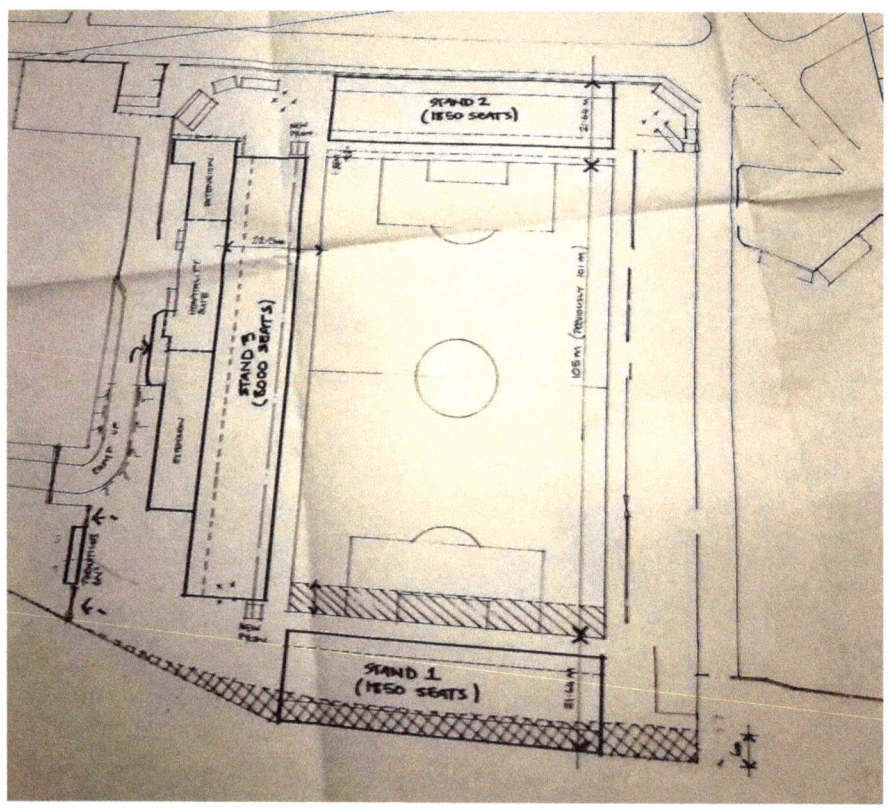

*This plan to redevelop Somerset Park envisaged stands being built at both ends and on the ground's northern axis.*

Proof that the search was broadening appeared on the front page of the *Ayr Advertiser* dated 15th April, 1998. The banner head line was:
SUPER STADIUM FOR UNITED?

Of course vigilant readers would have had their excitement tempered by the question mark. However the author had difficulty in suppressing positive emotions on first seeing a flysheet outside a newsagent's. It bore the legend **AYR UNITED MAY MOVE TO MONKTON.** My home village – surely it was too good to be true. The site mentioned in the story was Shields Farm, located close to Sandyford Toll on the Prestwick bypass. There was a proposal from Heritage Scotland, a subsidiary of the Barr organisation. It was fronted by Kenny MacLeod, who was an Ayr United director. In the world of new football stadia he was highly skilled in cutting through the swathe of planning regulations. In relation to Shields Farm outline plans were submitted for business, assembly and leisure use. In technical terms it was deemed to be a class four application. Amidst the plethora of potential difficulties was the fact that it was contrary to the local plan.

In September 1998 news emerged that a ban on out-of-town developments in the Heathfield district of the town was to be lifted. Twenty-two developments had been held in abeyance principally because the Scottish Office believed that the nearby roads would not be able to cope with the additional traffic, the most contentious factor being the roundabout at Whitletts. With plans now having been lodged for an upgrade to the roundabout, the applications in the pipeline could now be considered. The Shields Farm application was one of those stuck in limbo. Other key applications in the log jam included an ASDA superstore which would see the removal of their town centre outlet, several applications from companies associated with the Barr group to include a new business park, new office buildings, a leisure centre and a budget hotel development and a proposal from Alexander Sawmills for a retail warehouse, multiplex cinema and a restaurant.

Your average Ayr United supporter cared little for the fine detail of planning strategy or reports drawn up by road engineers. Together with the debate as to whether or not the contentious roundabout required an underpass it all paled into insignificance in comparison to the big question. Would Ayr United be getting a new stadium? Another consideration was the time factor. A draconian measure had been brought in whereby participation in the Scottish Premier League would require a stadium comprising a minimum of 10,000 seats. For the past twenty years the club had only ever played in the second or third tiers of Scottish football but as the 1998/99 season progressed the question of promotion became a realistic contingency. A 4-1 win at home to Clydebank on 14th November put the club on top of the First Division. In the event of maintaining top spot there would be no promotion at the season's end unless a new stadium could be built. Ground sharing on a temporary basis had already been ruled out as unacceptable by the Scottish Premier League. This was blatant hypocrisy on their part since Celtic had been permitted to play their home games at Hampden during season 1994/95. What were the alternatives? Redeveloping Somerset Park had already been deemed as impractical. Outline planning permission only had been granted on the Shields Farm site besides which there was speculation that the proximity to the Prestwick Airport flight path would make it a non starter. Old Toll had also been identified as a possible site for relocation. The piece of ground in question was a little way beyond the Holmston Roundabout on the A70 to Coylton. It was the former Scottish Power site. Some of the land was already owned by Barr Holdings and plans were drawn up but the idea had to be scrapped because it was not possible to buy an additional bit of ground which would have been necessary to accommodate what was planned. Regarding the options Mr Barr said: "The club have a number of options but no final decision can be taken by the board until all aspects of planning and support are fully clarified."

On 23rd November plans for a 10,000 seater stadium development got lodged for another site. This application was coupled with a proposal for a 120,000 square foot retail development in order to cross fund it. The location was at Old Lochside Road. On behalf of the council a spokesman said that the application would be considered by the strategic services committee in six weeks time. Time would prove this to be the thin end of a very considerable wedge. On 18th January, 1999, the council stated that they were awaiting information on the retail and traffic impact of the proposed development and that they hoped to deal with the application "as quickly as possible". The lack of a definitive timescale was frustrating.

On 20th January, 1999, the author phoned Roger Mitchell who was then the chief executive of the Scottish Premier League. With surprising ease I was put through to him. He started off by asking whether he should know me. Initially I stated that we were poles apart on what was good for Scottish football and I suggested meeting with him in order to gain clarification on certain points. He then asked me whom I was representing and I said myself. I then thought it prudent to give him a brief rundown of my involvement as an Ayr United historian, shareholder and supporter. His response was a suggestion that there would be no point in a meeting since our views were "diametrically opposed." My counter suggestion was that a meeting would be beneficial because I could give him a very good case for relaxing his policies. He then told me that he was getting phone calls and letters stating opposition to the 10,000 seater ruling every day and asked me whether I considered it reasonable that he should meet with everyone. I said: "No, but you should meet with me because I have a heavy emotional commitment in football. His reply was: "So you are saying that you should be a special case." I said yes then told him that I was getting embroiled in just what I did not want to get embroiled in i.e. discussing matters over the phone rather than face to face. He said: "You never hear the ten SPL chairmen complaining." I replied: "No wonder. They are protected in a cocoon." He said that his quotes in the media were not just his and that he could be sacked for stating a contrary view. Candidly he said that forty clubs was too many in Scotland and that clubs should be centred on the main centres of population of which he considered Ayr to be one. This was his response when I questioned him about his remark in the *Daily Mail* that there were too many clubs in Fife. My comeback to this was that nobody would support a merger between Raith Rovers and Dunfermline Athletic. He said that all appropriate parties had been consulted including supporters' chief Martin Rose. I pointed out to him that this gentleman was a Motherwell fan and that this club, being in the Premier League already, had a vested interest.

Mr Mitchell was fulsome in his praise of the clubs that had already developed their stadiums and I countered this by the impact created by debt. He re-emphasised his praise by saying that these clubs had been "willing to bite the bullet." Several times he said that he would have to get off the phone in order to prepare for a meeting the next day. Ultimately he asked me if I was satisfied. I replied: "No, I'm not satisfied." He then said: "Good afternoon sir." At this point the call terminated when I was vainly attempting to speak back.

In late January 1999 a further problem emerged. A new Ayrshire-wide strategy was adopted by South Ayrshire Council. The strategic services committee approved an initiative which railed against out-of-town shopping in favour of town centre sites. Ian Johnson, the structure plan officer, emphasised that applications for retail development at Heathfield would now have to be looked at in light of the new structure plan.

On 27th February a United for Heathfield campaign got launched at a public meeting in the Checkers Lounge Bar in New Road. This was a fan-led initiative under the leadership of John Dalton and the others in the group were John Mcdonald, Kevin McLelland, David Low, Duncan

McLean and myself. Around 200 people assembled in the lounge and in the course of vigorous discussion it was agreed that the campaign group would quiz every candidate for May's council and Scottish elections. The premise was simple. Candidates opposed to the stadium and retail complex would be named and Ayr United supporters would be urged not to vote for them. This was a lunchtime meeting prior to the Ayr United versus Hibs fixture that afternoon. A 3-1 defeat put the final nail in the hopes of winning the league besides which the sands of time had run out anyway. It was somewhat merciful. The notion of winning the league and not getting promotion due to the stadium criteria would have been too tough to contemplate. Yet the resolve to get a new stadium did not diminish. It was known that from 2000/01 the Premier League would be increased by two clubs to make it a twelve-club division. The top two in the First Division for 1999/2000 would pass into the Premier League (subject to the stadium criteria being met) with there being no relegation. With the club on course for a third place finish in the current season the prospect of finishing in the top two in 1999/2000 was far from fanciful. Unfortunately delivering the stadium in time was becoming increasingly fanciful.

United for Heathfield considered putting up candidates for the May 1999 local elections. It seemed a good idea until the realisation dawned that we could not vote on an issue in which we had what was clearly a vested interest. Nonetheless the campaigning work continued by way of canvassing politicians, local and national, and countering letters of opposition in the local newspapers.

Despite speculation that the planning application would be heard before the May elections the date was set for 30th June. Owing to the large public interest the venue was the Citadel Leisure Centre in South Harbour Street. On the night in question the large hall was close to capacity. A petition in support of the application had in excess of 8,000 signatures, most of which had been collected in Ayr High Street on the Saturday before the hearing. Further illustrative of the public mood was the fact that 864 letters of support had been received and just fifty-nine objections. However the buoyant mood was blunted when, prior to the hearing, it emerged that the council's planning officials had put together a 30-page document outlining the background to the application but which recommended rejection. They claimed that the retail element went against government guidelines aimed at limiting the number of out-of-town shopping centres. Take a walk around Heathfield today and you will quickly see that in the intervening years there has been a proliferation of retail outlets in that district. The document further stated that the retail element could be placed in the town centre. Beresford Terrace, Kyle Street and Damside were named as potential sites.

Planning hearings may be perceived as somewhat staid but this one had the characteristics of a pantomime. Interested parties took turns at standing before the packed assembly and giving their case for or against the application. Those in favour received uproarious applause and those against received booing and catcalls. Supporters of the application were given ten minutes in which to state their case. There was no such restriction on Director of Strategic Services Archie Harkness who spoke in opposition to the application for just over half an hour.

There was a sensational twist when Alex Cairns (Labour) moved to amend the Planning Department's recommendation for refusal. Margaret Toner (Conservative) seconded the motion. The cheering within the hall peaked only to be stifled in its infancy. This was because Andy Hill (Convenor) moved in favour of the original recommendation to refuse the application. The relief was almost tangible when he failed to find a seconder. Confusion arose. Ostensibly it appeared as if the application had been passed but it was not clear whether any conditions were attached. Bill Barr had even to intervene to get clarification on what had been agreed.

The meeting ran from 5.30pm until 7.20pm yet confusion was evident when people streamed out at the end of the hearing not knowing whether it was a victory or a defeat. South Ayrshire Council allayed the confusion by confirming that they had referred the application to the Scottish Executive, claiming that they were required to do so by law. It was now in the hands of Sarah Boyack, the Scottish Parliament's planning minister. This was bad news because it was known to involve a long process. Even at this juncture it was reasonably assumed that this would overrun the Scottish Premier League's deadline to fulfil the stadium criteria by 31st March, 2000. Regardless of what happened out on the pitch in 1999/2000 there would be no Premier League football in Ayr in 2000/01.

It was hoped that the stadium plans would be dealt with quickly by the civil servants in Edinburgh. This was a forlorn hope. The belief at the Citadel that there was some kind of victory was just a cruel deception. News that a public inquiry would now take place was as depressing as it was tedious. The inquiry got underway at the Citadel on 7th October. It was deemed to be a 'pre-hearing meeting'. The formal start took place on 13<sup>th</sup> December. Once more it was a process of parties for and against giving evidence. It became a spiral of meetings and counter meetings prior to a decision being announced on 3<sup>rd</sup> November, 2000.

After procrastination on a grand scale the decision was to allow planning permission for a new stadium at Heathfield but to refuse planning permission for the retail element. This was all but fatal since the retail element was essential to the cross funding. It was a curious decision in light of it being a single application. Moreover the knife was twisted with the imposition of £2.5 million planning gain to include the provision of land for a rail halt, the provision of a bus service from the town centre and payment towards roadworks including improvements to Whitletts Roundabout. The local football club was seriously expected to fund the town's infrastructure. The report even detailed the types of plants and shrubs to be used in the landscaping surrounding the stadium. Cycle lanes were required too. The esteemed planners would have been hard pressed to name any Scottish football stadium that already had provision for cyclists turning up. It was considered by the club's advisers that "the development may now not be workable." The word 'may' was a massive understatement. This was all at the behest of Sam Galbraith who was then the Scottish Environment minister. It was a terrible decision which flew in the face of 176 pages of evidence.

Of course there was a right to appeal. The appeal was duly lodged and it led to a quite extraordinary development in February 2002. That considerable passage of time had caused all or most supporters to have suffered from stadium fatigue. Surely the application was dead. Maybe not! The Court of Session quashed the Scottish Executive's decision because their Planning Division admitted that their case was "fatally flawed." With no opposition to the appeal the case was surely won. It did not work in that way. It only meant that the case was sent back to the Scottish Executive "for further consideration". In October 2002 Hugh Henry, who now had the environment brief, decided to stick with the original decision despite the admission that it was fatally flawed. In 2007 Mr Henry, then an MSP for Paisley South, expressed his delight when St.Mirren's relocation got ratified. From an Ayr perspective the only winner in 2002 was Old Lady Somerset.

## Chapter Fifteen

# Heathfield – Attempt Number Two

In November 2006 the Ayr United board wrote to the club's shareholders to advise that conditional contracts had been concluded for the sale of Somerset Park to Barratt Homes and for the purchase of a 20-acre site at Lochside Road. On the new site it was planned to build a Stadium, Sports and Business Campus with the work being completed in four phases. The planning applications had been lodged on 24th November. It was all dependent on planning permission being granted at two locations.

1. A residential development by Barratt at Somerset Park and on a 6-acre portion of the Heathfield site.

2. A mixed stadium, sports and business development by Ayr United on the remaining 14-acre portion of the Heathfield site.

There was a very important proviso.

"The project will not proceed unless both planning permissions are secured. In the event that the permissions are secured, Ayr United will remain at Somerset Park under a Licence to Occupy from Barratt until phase one of the project is complete and ready to accommodate the football club."

This time the driving force was not solely the hope of attaining Premier League football. In November 2006 that would have been a ridiculous aspiration. At the time the planning applications were lodged our latest result was a 1-0 defeat at home to Alloa Athletic and this was the first of six consecutive league defeats in Scottish football's third tier. In this less than illustrious sphere the club was on course to finish fifth in season 2006/07. During the second part of that campaign home league gates dipped to three figures on five occasions. A humbling seventh place finish was the club's lot in 2007/08.

Despite dispiriting on-field results the club was in good hands. On 4th September, 2003, Barr Holdings announced that it had sold its 77% stake in Ayr United. The purchaser was club director Donald Cameron. This made him the new owner, albeit that, being based in California, he did not become chairman at this time. Yet on 4th March, 2005, he did become the chairman, eventually yielding the chairmanship to his son Lachlan in 2008, a position he held until 2021.

The Cameron family cared deeply for Ayr United and it is beyond doubt that they always had the club's best interests at heart. Yet the major question in 2006 was just how a £15 million stadium could be funded. The answer was laid out in detail. The cost of purchasing the 14-acre Heathfield site plus the cost of constructing the stadium would be funded by the sale of Somerset Park. As regards the other part of the phase one development, which would include approximately 29,000 feet of commercial office space, it would require, in part, borrowing. The borrowing was deemed viable through obtaining revenue from the rent accrued from commercial leases of the office accommodation. Some funding would also be sought from sportscotland who trendily marketed their name in lower case. Up to 700 car parking spaces would be provided. The beginning of season 2008/09 was given as the earliest possible time for relocation to the new stadium. This project was put together by some agile brains, not least that of Iain Pearson who was the club's company secretary between 2005 and 2007 after which he remained a regular supporter. Sadly he passed away during the writing of this book.

Adjoining the stadium would be fifty-four flats and fifty-two houses comprising a mix of semi-detached and terraced homes. Thirty-four of the flats would comprise affordable housing. The commercial aspects were, of course, crucial to the success of the development but to the supporters the overwhelming interest was the stadium. It would have a capacity of 7,650 comprising 3,650 seats in the main West Stand, 3,000 seats in the East Stand and terracing provision to accommodate 1,000 standing spectators. The stadium dimensions would be 190 metres by 128 metres. The pitch would run on a north to south alignment. Floodlighting pylons, 29 metres in height, would be situated in each corner of the ground. With due allowance for the proximity of housing it was stipulated that these would only be used for matches. On the Somerset Park site 155 flats would be built by Barratt.

Chairman Donald Cameron said:

"In my opinion the announcement of the Ayr United stadium development is a watershed in the club's history. It's the beginning of a process that, when successful, will lead Ayr United to its rightful place as one of Scotland's major provincial football clubs."

His hint of rhetoric did not mask the fact that the project seemed viable. Vice-chairman Mark Meehan stressed the community benefits:

"We believe this announcement will mark the beginning of an exciting and ground breaking era in the history of Ayr United. This ambitious stadium development will deliver the town of Ayr and the wider community of Ayrshire, football and sports facilities of a standard which will restore pride and put Ayrshire back on the map as a centre of excellent sports resources."

There was substance to his reference to the community benefits. One such was the provision of half-sized indoor pitches which the general public would be permitted to use.

Objections to the stadium part of the application were predictable but reasonable. These were typically in relation to traffic congestion, the possibility of parking in adjacent streets, light pollution and noise pollution. It being an overgrown site there was also a concern about the loss of wildlife.

Even with due allowance for the complexity of the application, the process was once more tortuous. The rigours of the first attempt to relocate to Heathfield left many feeling embittered. There was an undercurrent of cynicism which could have been encapsulated in the saying 'here we go again'. It was a negativity born of experience. No one doubted that the project had been brilliantly conceived yet when the fans discussed it the conversation would invariably induce the viewpoint "I'll believe it when I see it." True to the public perception delay followed delay and each meeting was followed by a counter meeting. Whether through petulance or not there was a feeling that Ayr United were getting picked upon. Fans could easily rhyme off the names of other clubs who had relocated with nothing like the same difficulty.

On 31st January, 2008, there was a sudden change of mood. South Ayrshire Council granted conditional planning permission on that date. Kenny MacLeod had put in a power of work in the initial attempt to move to Heathfield. By 2008 he was no longer an Ayr United director but he was actively engaged in this latest application through his involvement with developers Rockwood. In response to the positive decision he said this at the meeting:

> "These applications represent a watershed in the history of Ayr United in that they offer a real opportunity to deliver 21$^{st}$ century facilities for the benefit of the club and the people of South Ayrshire."

In his capacity as the club's managing director Lachlan Cameron issued the following statement:

> "This morning the club and our supporters took a major step forward to realising modern purpose-built 21st century facilities at our new home at Heathfield. The approval of these applications bring us to the start of our new beginning. The club can progress from here and be a competitive force. We look forward to agreeing the relevant planning agreements with the council in early course. Until these are resolved we are unable to confirm a timetable for the stadium but continue to strive to open phase one in time for the 2009/10 centenary season. Allied to substantial investment in office and business space and the provision of considerable affordable housing units we believe that these combined applications are of significant merit."

Team manager Brian Reid was equally buoyant:

> "I am really delighted that the stadium has been approved. It really is a great boost for the club. There will be excellent new facilities including a training pitch and hopefully this might help attract even more quality players to Ayr United when they see what the club is doing."

This most welcome news was perceived as an absolute certainty that the move would occur. Note Lachlan Cameron's reference to "our new home at Heathfield." The home shirts for season 2008/09 carried lettering showing  Somerset Park 1888 – 2009 as did the programme cover. This was in the belief that 2008/09 would be the last season at the old ground. Yet although we were stuck with that lettering for the whole season that campaign had barely got underway when devastating news got delivered. On 22$^{nd}$ August, 2008, by which time three league fixtures had been completed, it was announced that Barratt had, to quote their spokesman, "withdrawn from the project". Further enquiries to Barratt brought forth clarification that "the council's planning agreements on social affordable housing were unworkable." There is an old saying that coming events cast their shadow before. This alludes to a phone call I made to council leader Hugh Hunter in the hope of finding out why, since planning permission had been granted, the project seemed no nearer getting started. It was to his credit that he spoke to me since I was not the applicant and it was further to his credit that he gave a straight answer. Quite simply the council wanted more social housing on the Somerset Park site than Barratt wished to build. The August development was an endorsement that there was no scope for negotiation. Ironically Mr Hunter had been in attendance at the inaugural United for Heathfield meeting aimed at promoting the first attempt to move to that area. Here is a further irony. When the application had been approved in January 2008, Nan McFarlane, the panel chairwoman, made this comment:

"I welcome the development of a new football stadium for Ayr United, offices and parking. A higher level of socially affordable housing would have been welcome but this percentage will have a very positive impact on the demand for housing in the area."

The council denied causing this devastating turn of events. David Anderson had been chief executive of South Ayrshire Council for four months. His response was:

"South Ayrshire Council's regulatory panel approved the application subject to the legal agreement. The council has been working with Barratt, Ayr United, registered social landlords and others to progress the agreement in accordance with the council's planning for socially affordable housing. We believe that significant progress had been made between the legal representatives of the parties involved and indeed that matters were close to being concluded. Barratt chose to withdraw as negotiations were still ongoing, while the council continue to work on the project with Ayr United."

Old Lady Somerset, being inanimate, was not in a position to make a quote but she had once more defied the bulldozers.

Lachlan Cameron had succeeded his father as chairman on 10th March, 2008. He was now in an unforeseen situation. His hope was that a developer could be found to step into Barratt's shoes. The difficulty here was that 2008 was the year in which the credit crunch occurred. On being asked whether it was viable to stay at Somerset Park he said:

"In a word no. It really is a non starter. The club has investigated this option with professional advice in years past and concluded that there was no viable option for staying at Somerset Park."

*It was anticipated that relocation would take place to this stadium in 2009*

*This is the programme cover for our last home match of 2008/09. All season the wording SOMERSET PARK 1888 – 2009 was shown, albeit that hopes of moving had long since been crushed.*

*Chapter Sixteen*

# The Hub

*The Hub in all its beauty in 2023.*

Rogue ownership of a football club can be detrimental to the point of being fatal. In contrast Ayr United have been blessed by having owners who, in addition to having great business acumen, have also had an emotional attachment to the club. Bill Barr fitted that profile in addition to his successors Donald Cameron then Lachlan Cameron. The next successor was David Smith. Mr Smith had been a supporter since his days of being a schoolboy in Girvan. On 13th December, 2019, he became a director and at a board meeting on 7th July, 2020, he was voted in as vice-chairman. His next step in the club hierarchy came on 12th January, 2021, when it was announced that he had acquired a majority shareholding in the club and he was now the new owner and chairman. Owner✓ : chairman✓ : supporter✓ – all boxes ticked! Lachlan Cameron had been forthright in stating that he was willing to sell the club but he was equally adamant in his determination that it would only be sold to the right person. David Smith clearly fitted that profile. This was the man who introduced a word hitherto virtually unheard of in conversation between Ayr United supporters. Infrastructure! This infrastructure was addressed in two constituent parts. 1. Getting the right people into the right jobs. 2. Getting modern facilities built. The fans bought into his way of thinking and there was unanimous support for what he was trying to achieve. As Managing Director of construction firm Ashleigh (Scotland) Limited he possessed expertise which could be deployed to the benefit of Ayr United. Moreover he had begun that process prior to becoming the club owner, albeit that he was a director.

Mr Smith was unhappy with some aspects of the image of Somerset Park. For example the club offices were of portakabin construction in the car park. This was just one legacy of the historic desire to relocate. Portakabins had no connotations of permanency but the realisation had since dawned that the club's future would be at Somerset Park. Rats being discovered underneath the offices comprised the most graphic evidence that something had to be done. The overall image was potentially detrimental when these premises were being used to conduct negotiations for new players. To put it mildly it was not a good look. Mr Smith's firm had an inspirational motto; Raising Standards. He was soon to employ that principle to Ayr United with spectacular effect. In an *Ayrshire Post* interview he said:

> "Football is full of chancers who say they will do this or do that and I never wanted to be one of those people but until you actually deliver something it will only ever be noise or chat. So I was determined to come in and deliver something quickly and make people sit up and take note."

He made a similar point in conversation with the author when he said that he would never say that he would do something without first of all being sure that the resources were there to deliver. He was true to his word.

Denham Youd were the architects charged with the responsibility of designing a new building aimed at "upgrading the public frontage to the stadium entrance and featuring a new club shop, reception area and social facility, all to benefit the local community." The planning application was submitted on 7th July, 2020.

The site, at the junction of Tryfield Place and Back Hawkhill Avenue, had been acquired by the club in 1980. At that time there was a cottage on the site. By 2020 it was still there but it was disused. Planning permission was now being sought to demolish the cottage and the adjoining garage together with the adjacent club shop and office accommodation. A new club shop, reception area, office accommodation and a social facility would take its place.

Quite apart from the practical consideration there was the question of image. On approaching the ground the sight of a ruinous cottage and some portakabins was less than alluring. In contrast the new facility would invigorate the image by being alluring in every detail. Of course there was the substantial question about whether or not planning permission would be obtained. Historical precedent gave every indication that this could be a tough nut to crack. This time it was different. Approval was given on 30th July, barely more than three weeks after the plans had been submitted. The reason for the decision was formally worded: "The siting and design of the development hereby approved is considered to accord with the provisions of the development plan and there is no significant adverse impact on the amenity of neighbouring land and buildings."

The recommendation for agreement went so far as to praise the aesthetic nature of what had been proposed: "It is considered that whilst presenting as a differentially modern design solution relative to the existing house and the prevailing general character of dwellings nearby, its single-storey form retains a basic general residential scale; meanwhile the application's site's distinct situation at the street's end causes proposal form and design not to present as interrupting any discernible rhythm of form or continuity of streetscape, nor is it therefore considered incongruous. Instead it is considered to contribute a degree of visual interest at the locus and specifically insofar as it presents an active frontage wrapping around the corner of a presently barren island of public realm to the overall benefit of visual amenity at the locality." Translating this planning-speak into colloquial English it simply meant that The Hub would enhance the area.

The decision to approve the application was made without a site visit due to the Scottish Government's advice on containing the spread of Covid 19. This leads neatly to a most relevant point. No matter the speed of construction it could not be known just when the facility would be in a thriving state. In the summer of 2020 we lived in a world of social distancing and face masks. After playing at Dundee on 10th March, 2020, our next match was away to Albion Rovers on 6th October, comprising a gap of 210 days without a match. This comprises the second longest spell without a game in the club's history. It is beaten only by the war-induced barren spell of 5 years 71 days between 1st June, 1940, and 11th August, 1945. Even when football did eventually resume in October 2020 no paying spectators were admitted, a situation that was to persist for the entire season. Yet there was no weakening in the resolve to construct The Hub. Although no one knew quite when, it was reasonable to take it for granted that Covid 19 would gradually subside.

Construction was started by Ashleigh on 4th May, 2021. Six weeks later the frame arrived and from this point onwards it was gratifying to see it gradually taking shape. The finished article was every bit as attractive as it appeared on the drawing board. Yet there was an addition to the original plans. In August a separate planning application was lodged for an outdoor fan zone and beer garden. Approval was granted.

Outwith the public eye further renovative work comprised modernisation to the boardroom, all done in a manner which retained the traditional features. The most attractive of these traditional features is the line of four stained glass windows showing the Auld Brig, Burns Cottage, Greenan Castle and the Heads of Ayr. These were gifted in 1935 in commemoration of Ayr United's silver jubilee. The donor was Andrew Wright, a club director who founded a glazing firm which still flourishes today. Had either of the abortive moves to Heathfield taken place the plan was to uninstal these windows then reinstal them in the new location. Somerset Park is the only ground in Scotland to have stained glass windows. Celtic Park has leaded windows but there is a distinction between those and stained glass windows. What is the distinction? The answer is outwith the author's area of expertise!

Having touched on the internal of the boardroom let us now revert to topic and discuss the internal of The Hub. The bar was named Cameron's

Bar. David Smith picked this name because Lachlan Cameron, Ayr United's longest serving chairman of all time, had been so reasonable to deal with when transferring the ownership of the club. Within the bar the theme was overwhelmingly one of nostalgia, albeit that the fixtures and fittings had all the trappings of modernity. Murals and photographs of legendary teams and players adorned the walls. The tables gave the illusion of having old match programmes scattered over them. In reality these were scans held in place by glass.

*The Hub table tops, each dedicated to a club legend and beautifully adorned with programme covers.*

Cameron's Bar had a trial opening night on 2nd December, 2021, and I had the privilege of being one of the invited guests. On going to pay for my first pint in the new facility David Smith quickly intervened to say: "It's on me." Thank you Mr Smith! The first match day opening occurred on Boxing Day. Covid had once more intensified thereby creating a restricted attendance of 472 for a 2-0 win over Raith Rovers. By the third week in January the requirement for restricted attendances was lifted and from this point onwards Cameron's Bar flourished. It removed the requirement to visit the nearby Hawkhill Bowling Club for a pre-match drink. Well, not quite! The facility immediately became so popular that people had to be politely turned away long before kick-off time.

It would be remiss to wind up this chapter on The Hub while omitting an acknowledgement of the sterling work done by the scheme's project manager Kenny Blair.

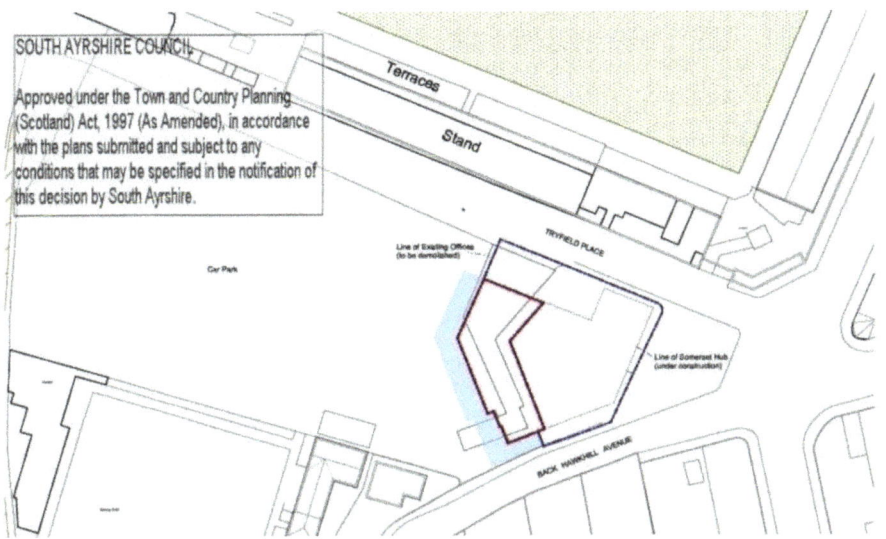

*Approved is the key word in this image. The approval is in respect of the beer garden.*

*Chapter Seventeen*

# The North Stand

You may recall the television game show Family Fortunes. It worked on a very simple premise whereby the contestants had to guess the top answer to a general question posed to 100 people in a survey. Let us now paraphrase this concept to imagine 100 Ayr United supporters being asked which ground improvement they would most like to see at Somerset Park. Beyond all shadow of a doubt the top answer would have been covering the north terrace. On the evening of 9th June, 2022, a club vision night was held in The Hub. Prior to the event some fans speculated that this particular improvement would be on the agenda. Yet to the older and more battle weary amongst us the very idea of it seemed too good to be true. The scepticism was born out of experience rather than negativity. However the plans rolled out to the fans that evening confirmed that this much craved development was, subject to planning permission, going to happen. These were the main points:

A North Stand would be built comprising 748 seats in front of which the terracing would be covered by a cantilevered roof canopy. A wheelchair seating zone would be integrated.

The structure would contain a new hospitality suite with a capacity for 170 guests. This would necessitate the demolition of the Ally MacLeod Suite.

The new hospitality suite would feature a corporate facility for the benefit of companies of varying size.

Purpose built offices would be built within the new stand with the consequence that the club's operations centre would be removed from The Hub to the new offices. The Hub offices would be retained for use by the Ayr United Football Academy.

Black sheet metal would be used as a background effect to the entrance which would have Ayr United Football Club spelled out in white glazed brick.

The ten existing parking bays adjoining the Ally MacLeod Suite would be retained but revamped and new parking bays would be constructed. Additional provision would be made for disabled parking bays.

In common with The Hub the architects were again Denham Youd and Ashleigh would carry out the construction. Engineers Clancy Consulting would also have a pivotal role. With commendable historical awareness Denham Youd mentioned the following in a planning statement: "The main stand at Somerset Park was designed by the much celebrated architect and engineer of football stadiums Archibald Leitch. We have tried to be mindful of this in our design." It was quite natural that the pertinent question of cost would arise. When the question did arise David Smith had an instant answer. He was willing to underwrite the seven-figure cost. Notwithstanding that it was a big project he managed to sum it up in one word – "transformational". In saying this he was perhaps mindful of the fact that, when he was a lad, he used to stand on the north terrace with his father and his uncle.

The planning application was received by South Ayrshire Council on 11th July, 2022. Would it be approved? Ayr United supporters had grown less fearful of planning procedures since the construction of The Hub but that did not totally diminish a 'wait and see' mindset. Even to the untrained eye it looked as if the application could not fail. The architects had covered the minute detail of every conceivable aspect, right down to the minutiae of the construction of the seats. It helped too that the council received 146 representations of support for the project from the general public. Only one representation counted as an objection. This was despite that particular representation offering support for the development. These communications highlighted the following benefits:

Improved facilities would enhance the experience of spectators by creating an attractive, new, safer and user friendly entrance and stadium. It would be a well used community facility which would ensure the ongoing operation of the club.

There would be economic benefits by way of increased investment and the retention of economic activity within the town. The potential for job creation would also exist and the facility could comprise an attraction for visitors to the area.

There would be enhanced visual amenity. The proposed North Stand would be aesthetically pleasing while retaining the heritage of the area and possibly acting as a catalyst in the regeneration of the surrounding area.

There would be no adverse impact on nearby residential properties.

Benefits would accrue by way of income for Ayr United in addition to community benefits and the likelihood of raising the profile of the town.

Of course with a project of this size the input by the associated professionals was all important but the public perception, as illustrated by the aforementioned bullet points, added weight to the case. Yet the first attempt to move to Heathfield had failed in face of what was a complete avalanche of public support. Mercifully there was no such anguish in 2022. On 2$^{nd}$ September approval was granted. This paved the way for construction to commence in 2023 with completion scheduled for 2024.

The prospect of changing the face of the north terrace will evoke memories, most especially amongst the ranks of the senior citizens within the Ayr United fanbase. Gone is the Black and White Shop. Gone is the half-time scoreboard that had the hallmark of being a Heath Robinson contraption. Gone too is the half-time migration through the north terrace to change ends. Your writer's earliest memory of Somerset Park is standing with my father on that particular terrace in 1959/60, albeit that he refused to take me to some games that season on the grounds that the crowds were too big and I was too small. The visits of Rangers and Celtic induced the most categoric refusals. However it is perhaps being a bit over emotional to write about the north terrace in such a way as to imply that it is on the point of disappearing. On completion of the grand scale renovation of this part of the ground the standing areas will still exist and it is most commendable that the team of architects possessed both the skill and the willingness to blend tradition with modernity.

The fickle nature of football makes it difficult to foretell what the future will hold but one prophecy can be made with certainty. Old Lady Somerset will not be budged from her home of longstanding.

 *This dedicated bunch carry out maintenance work at Somerset Park on a voluntary basis. Rear left to right: Ronnie Hainey and Jim Mitchell. Front left to right: Adam Merry, Brian Hawkes and Alasdair Malcolm.*

*Jason Waddell – the groundsman who does a fantastic job in ensuring that the pitch is of lush quality.*

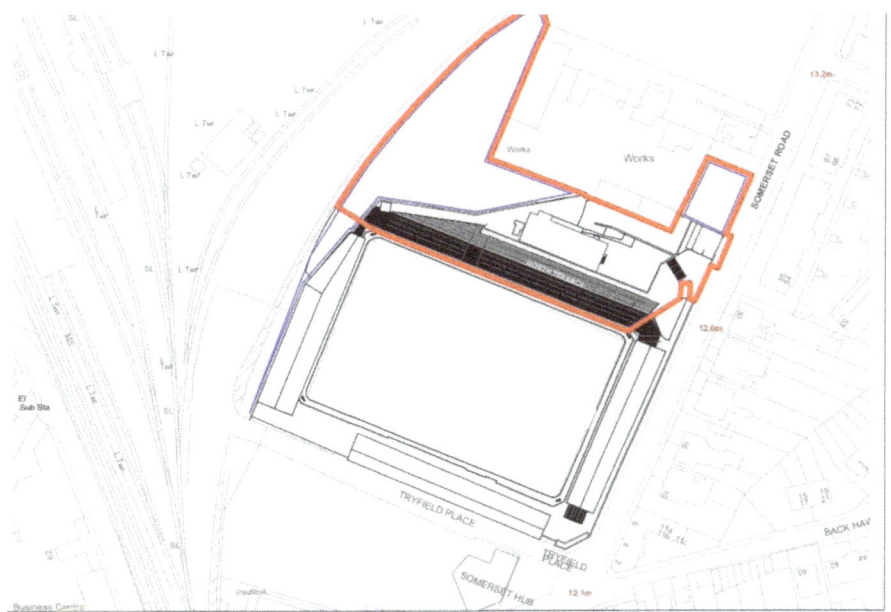

*The North Stand layout as seen on the drawing board.*

*The view from the tunnel.*

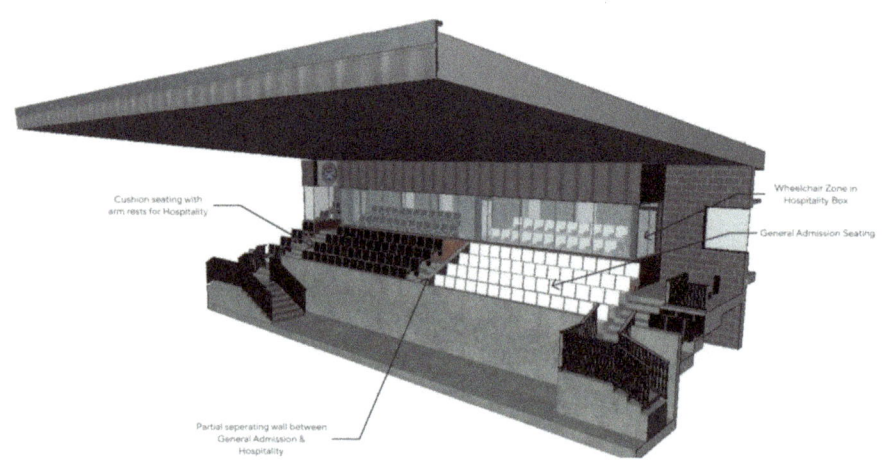

*A cross section of the additional seating.*

*The side elevation.*

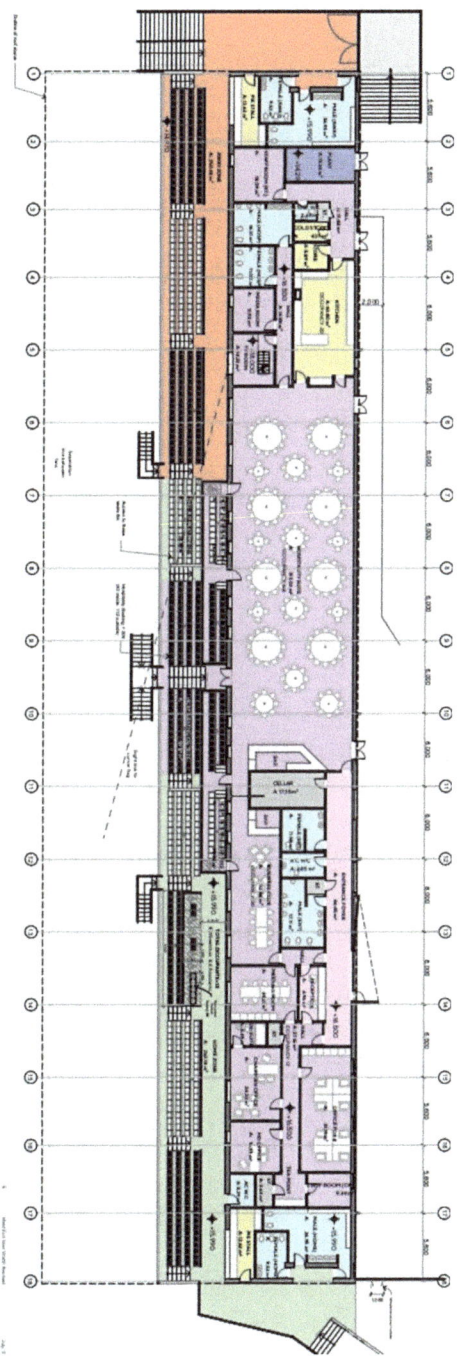

The internal layout of the North Stand.

Ayr United versus Queen's Park on the Friday evening of 19th April, 1957. This photograph encapsulates what it was like to stand on the north terrace in the pouring rain. Trench coats and caps are prevalent enough to convey the image of a uniform. Note too that the policeman's coat is billowing in the wind. The spectators huddled at the foot of the half-time scoreboard appear to have an optimistic hope that this structure will offer some shelter, however scant. Peter Price (far left) is in the act of scoring in a 4-4 draw. The wisdom of covering the north terrace is crystal clear in this image.

The entrance.

*David Smith*

# Index